'Dr Judi Newman's book deeply resonated with me. Her use of real-life examples and personalised experiences brought her insights to life and made a lasting impact on my growth as a leader. The authenticity and relevance of each story inspired me to reflect more deeply on my own leadership journey.'
Kara Krehlik, Principal, Australia

'An essential read for school leaders searching to elevate their impact beyond authority. Grounded in neuroscience, Judi reveals how learning and behaviour drive transformational leadership. She provides principals with the toolkit to inspire change, build cohesive teams, and nurture future leaders – while deepening their own professional growth and practice.'
Simon Bailey, Headmaster, Australia

'Judi has crafted a powerful guide that blends neuroscience and leadership. This book helps school leaders grow others while deepening their own impact.'
**Linda Galloway, School Supervisor,
Colonel, National Assistant Commander, Australian Army Cadets**

'Leadership is influence in action – and in schools, it's built through visible, everyday interactions that shape culture and connection. In *Influence*, Dr Judi Newman offers a powerful blend of neuroscience and practice, showing that effective leadership integrates both cognition and emotion. She reminds us that leadership is defined by moments of impact. This book invites you to create the space to shape your own leadership identity, offering insights that are both deeply informative and empoweringly practical.'
**Dr Barbara Watterston, CEO, Australian Council
for Educational Leaders**

'Judi's book stands as a masterful contribution to the field, elegantly illuminating leadership through a sophisticated neuroscience perspective. Her thoughtfully crafted 12 leadership attributes are not merely grounded in robust research but offer genuinely practical guidance for today's educational leaders navigating complex challenges.'
Professor Ken Purnell, NeuroEducation, CQ University

'Amid rising expectations for educational leaders, Dr Judi Newman delivers a breakthrough blend of neuroscience and leadership, specifically designed for a new generation of practitioners.'
**Nicole Regush, Associate Superintendent,
Catholic Independent Schools of the Vancouver Archdiocese, Canada**

'Dr Judi Newman is a brilliant thinker and engaging speaker whose insights captivated 1100 educational leaders at the uLead Conference in Banff, Canada. Her book is a must-read for anyone looking to lead with purpose and inspire transformation.'
Kristy Smith, Principal, Bermuda

'In an otherwise changing world, one thing remains certain – our need to know more about ourselves. Dr Judi Newman expertly takes us on a different journey with two open questions: how does the brain learn and how can such insight be embraced by leaders?'
Professor Stephen Dobson, Vice-rector, Norwegian University of Science and Technology

'Grounded in neuroscience research and enriched by experience, Dr Newman bridges the science of how we think and learn with the everyday realities of school leadership. As a fellow educational leader, her work is both validating and deeply inspiring.'
Associate Professor Julie Jhun, California State University, Dominguez Hills, USA

'Judi has crafted a book that all leaders will relate to. The insights about leadership influence go far beyond schools.'
Dr Justin James Kennedy, Institute of Organisational Neuroscience, Germany

Influence

How Educational Leaders Transform Thinking to Inspire, Unite and Deliver

DR JUDI NEWMAN

Published in 2025 by Amba Press, Melbourne, Australia
www.ambapress.com.au

© Judi Newman 2025

All rights reserved. No part of this book may be reproduced or transmitted in any form or by any means, electronic or mechanical, including photocopying, recording or by any information storage and retrieval system, without prior permission in writing from the publisher.

Cover design: Tess McCabe
Internal design: Amba Press
Editor: Andrew Campbell

ISBN: 9781923403222 (pbk)
ISBN: 9781923403239 (ebk)

A catalogue record for this book is available from the National Library of Australia.

CONTENTS

Foreword — vii
Preface — xi
Acknowledgments — xii
Introduction — 1

Part 1: Leadership and the Science — 9

Part 2: The 12 Leadership Attributes — 51

Leadership Attribute 1: Humility — 59
Leadership Attribute 2: Integrity — 67
Leadership Attribute 3: Strength — 74
Leadership Attribute 4: Clarity — 78
Leadership Attribute 5: Positivity — 89
Leadership Attribute 6: Connectedness — 102
Leadership Attribute 7: Appreciation — 110
Leadership Attribute 8: Collaboration — 115
Leadership Attribute 9: Communication — 121
Leadership Attribute 10: Purpose — 130
Leadership Attribute 11: Challenge — 138
Leadership Attribute 12: Autonomy — 146

Part 3: Influence Strategies **151**

I Is for Interpersonals	153
N Is for Needs	157
F Is for Fortitude and Boundaries	162
L Is for Leadership Strength	164
U Is for Understanding Bias	169
E Is for Emotion	175
N Is for Neuroplasticity	179
T Is for Tradition and Culture	187
I Is for Intentional Conversations	191
A Is for Accountability	193
L Is for Likeability	202
Afterword	205
References	206

FOREWORD

This book is a master class about *influence* where it matters most, with educational leaders in schools. It embraces the most current neuroscience to elucidate *how* to implement the most impactful leadership attributes.

At a time when leading teams are under pressure from constant change, complexity, and competing demands, there has never been a better time for mastering the determining factor in whether organisations merely function or flourish, namely influence.

In a highly engaging and accessible style, the book combines research, theory, and detailed applications to cultivate the kind of leaders the world needs today.

That's why *Influence: How Educational Leaders Transform Thinking to Inspire, Unite and Deliver* could not be more critical.

As an applied neuroscientist and medical doctor, I founded the First Standardized Database of Human Brain Function and Behavior, which comprises over a million datasets, 300 publications, and collaborations with researchers in 10 countries. The key outcomes focused on the dynamics of unconscious emotions, intuition, conscious feelings, and biases that influence rational decision-making and behaviours. Through this lens, I saw that the closer we get to the mechanism of action, the greater the influence and impact of the outcome.

Dr Judi Newman's research and this book judiciously apply what is known about the brain's mechanisms of decision-making and behaviours. Her work reveals significant deep leadership insights through an applied integrated neuroscience lens.

I've had the privilege of watching Judi's work unfold from the thesis research stage to her working with school and system leadership teams in the field. Our first conversations began when she was a principal herself, her work evolving from leading a school to delivering international keynotes, and now serving as a thought leader.

She brings a rare blend of lived experience and scientific knowledge to the field of educational leadership, bridging theory and practice. She views science through the eyes of an educator, making connections and drawing on her own leadership experience to create meaning and contextualise insights into human motivation, learning, and influence. Judi doesn't just understand leadership theory, she lives and breathes the real-world challenges that school leaders face every day. Her background in neuroscience adds an extraordinary depth, translating brain-based research into practical leadership tools that can shift thinking, culture, and outcomes.

There is a disconnect between what neuroscience shows and what organisations often do. Judi shows you how to close that gap by sharing evidence-based practice. She unpacks 12 leadership attributes and the DISCO framework to apply and strengthen influence, both personally and interpersonally, answering the pressing question of how to elevate energy, emotion and intellect to inspire a change in thinking.

She shows how influential leaders don't rely on authority or their positional badge, but they create the conditions for trust, rapport, and clarity. They are thought-shapers, meaning-makers, and culture-shifters, and above all, they are intentional in how they present themselves and bring others along with them.

Without neuroplastic changes in the brain over time, there is limited learning and behavioural change; therefore, this book highlights the importance of leadership as a highly relational process. Through stories grounded in science the reader can identify with the concepts and make their own connections.

What sets this book apart from other leadership books is the way it explains the 'how and why' behind our thinking and behaviour. To understand influence requires an understanding of our emotions, how we think, feel, learn, and remember. Keying into the neurological and psychological motivational triggers inherent in all individuals is essential for inspiring teams.

This is about leadership that transforms people and, in the process, transforms you.

Whether you lead a school, boardroom, or team, this book will transform the way you lead in a world where we need leaders who can inspire others to be braver, kinder, and bolder in their leadership, while also fostering renewed confidence in their ability to lead with impact.

It will remind you of the extraordinary power you hold as a leader and how you can strengthen that influence with ground-breaking implications.

Dr Evian Gordon, MD, PhD
Founder of the First International Human Brain Database
Chief Medical Officer of Total Brain, a Sondermind Company
Fellow of The American Institute of Stress

PREFACE

INSPIRE – UNITE – DELIVER

Leadership is about influence, not just authority. Who we are is how we lead. This book is about amplifying influence by strengthening leadership and learning impact through a neuroscience lens.

Without neuroplastic changes in the brain over time, there is limited learning and behaviour change. Leadership success is therefore directly tied to an understanding of the brain in regard to how we learn, think, feel and remember. Thinking is different from learning. When we think we fire neural networks but it is not until we wire neural networks that we learn, so for behaviour change to occur we need to move from knowing to doing.

Influential leadership can be viewed through a lens that addresses how humans respond to threat and social exclusion and should incorporate what we know about how a brain rewires. Explore how to boost your influence to inspire, unite and deliver by changing thinking for new behaviours for improved success, performance and wellbeing. This book is for those who want to inspire and build other leaders and, through that process, transform themselves.

Dr Judi Newman

ACKNOWLEDGMENTS

Always first, Kelvin and Woollee. You are my everything. Nothing is real until I share it with you.

Thank you to Professor Ken Purnell for your mentorship and Dr Evian Gordon for your encouragement.

To the principals who have trusted me to work with them: I have learnt so much from you.

INTRODUCTION

In the first few seconds of meeting someone we judge them by their trustworthiness, warmth and credibility. These instinctive emotional responses are rooted in our deeply held beliefs, fears and priorities, and often shape our perception of others until there is evidence to support another view. We can learn from the insights of neuroscience why this might be the case.

The brain has changed very little over the past 50,000 years, evolving to move, connect and problem-solve in a hunter-gather world. In essence, we share very much the same neural architecture as our Stone Age ancestors; however, we navigate a vastly different world of convenience, disconnection and relative comfort. Despite the modern context, our brain remains hardwired to detect threat, and this has significant implications for leadership behaviours and our ability to influence others. The primitive software affects how we perceive tone, language and interpersonal behaviour. These elements will either uplift the influence of the intellect, emotion and energy, to inspire the engagement of others, or leave a defensive wake. Leadership is a social influence occurring through biological processes manifesting in the brain that appeal to our inner motivations (Feser, 2016). This book explores how a deeper understanding of the brain through a neuroscience lens can strengthen our ability to influence, connect and inspire with greater impact.

Leadership is like love. You can say I love you or believe you are leading, but unless you see it in your behaviours and others feel an impact, it is only intent. Leadership is about doing. Leadership is but a moment, defined by an interaction that is influential. Listening to hundreds of leadership stories, I recognised that they had some shared threads. Those moments were more than a learning; they were more than a memory. They embodied a positive connection that revealed an emotion, which inspired an insight or change in thinking. Inspirational leadership moments are like neurotransmitters. They fire and ignite a key message for change.

Many of the leadership moments people have shared with me have a protective and service theme. Perhaps this is because the first role of the brain is to detect threat and keep us safe. Psychologists call this the 'social contract'. Some neuroscientists suggest that in the Stone Age, the strongest male was chosen as the leader and their key role was to protect the tribe. In return, they received the pick of the meat cuts, first choice of partner, and a say in most of their key choices and decisions. In modern organisations, gender has little to do with effective leadership, but there are similarities with the Stone Age leader in that the leader tends to be of strong character and is granted privileges to align with their pay grade and accountability, such as an office, parking space, and higher salary. The social contract theory would imply that if the CEO or school principal does not protect the team, then their right to those privileges will be rescinded. Thus, leadership and protection and service go hand in hand. In fact, leadership through a neuroscience lens can be captured in the words 'protect, serve and grow'.

The first time I encountered such leadership through the lens of protection and care of others was a moment early in my career. I was a second-year teacher in a high school and I was preparing for my inspection. All Queensland teachers at the time had to demonstrate their teaching expertise in their second year of teaching by being observed by two senior inspectors who travelled the state. This was a high-stakes job interview because if you passed, you went from probation to a fully registered teacher. On the day of my inspection, I prepared an engaging lesson and was advised by Mike Maher, one of the inspectors, to attend a debrief at 11am that same morning.

Sitting at my desk in the staffroom, I looked at the clock, and to my absolute dismay, I saw that it was ten past eleven. I had allowed myself to get distracted and absorbed in what I was doing. My heart was racing as I hurried to Block K, a long walk through the school, thinking I had blown it. Who would be silly enough to be late for their first big job interview? As I rushed in, Mike saw me and before I could speak, said, 'I am sorry, Judi, I gave you the wrong time – my fault. Please come in.' I was so nervous with impression management and inexperience, and confused by the unexpected response, that I didn't respond. The interview went well, and it wasn't until the next day that I realised that Mike had protected me. He showed a moment of influential leadership that would stay with me for the rest of my career. He made the decision to support me, rather than correct me, and on reflection it was very kind of him, because being held accountable at that critical time would have crushed me. He put my needs over his. He gave something of himself that day that was a gift. No one else noticed, but it made a huge difference to me. I never had the opportunity to thank him, and he passed away many years ago, but I am hoping that wherever he is, he knows he inspired me through his role-modelling that day. His influence in that one brief moment, with that one small act, changed my whole outlook on leadership. I now understood that effective leaders inspire and serve others. They allow others to shine.

About this book

This book is a summary of the findings of my PhD research, and is relevant for senior leadership development and the transmission of middle leaders from accidental managers into confident strategic leaders. Each section has been dotted with stories to show leadership in practice and incorporates studies to share the research, followed by the implications drawn from that evidence base. More importantly, each chapter includes practical strategies I have called tools that can be applied the next day.

The introduction outlines the nature of the book and my personal connection with the content. Part 1 unpacks the neuroscience that underpins leadership behaviours, learning and influence, and Part 2 introduces the 12 leadership attributes that inspire trust, rapport and growth in others. Part 3 outlines influence strategies informed by psychology and neuroscience that enable a leader to be an agent of change and a master communicator. There is limited change in behaviour and learning without neuroplastic changes in the brain over time, so this section explores ways to get people to do what you want them to do without a big stick.

Over the nine months in the research phase of my PhD, I shadowed high-performing secondary school principals in large schools and recorded everything they did and said. I interviewed them, asking, 'How do you inspire your team to bring out their best performance?' And I interviewed their team, asking, 'How does a leader inspire you to perform at your best?'

I share my findings in this book and show that an understanding of the brain is the missing link in order to redefine effective leadership. Many studies across industry, business and education agree on the characteristics and attributes that make an effective leader, but they don't always explain the why. Why do some leaders inspire us to perform at our best and why do other leaders trigger us into threat mode and make us feel defensive and resistant? Some leaders are able to draw out our best selves and make us shine, while others seem to shut us down and make us act small.

Insights and learnings from many years of lived experience as a former high school principal, executive coach and corporate consultant build on the empirical research that informs this work. This is not surprising, as a fundamental principle of neuroscience is that our brain is neuroplastic and changes form in response to our experience and learning over time. So, a combination of both lived experience in context and academic learning is essential for hardwiring of expertise. You can't become an expert overnight or by just reading a book. The more expert we become, the more connected and efficient our neural networks become, which sharpens our expertise and builds schemas that allow us to make decisions informed by our heart, gut and head combined. This concept is dependent on the finding that we have around 86 billion neurons in our brain, around 40 thousand in our heart, and 500 million in our gut (Gordon, 2020). The key is knowing when to make decisions with all three and when we require a more reasoned head space. If you are reading this book, I am guessing you have a combination of lived experience and academic reading, so you will be able to make the connections easily, as you have a range of neural chains (or schemas) already consolidated to your long-term memory around educational leadership.

To gain further insight into what effective leadership looks like, I interviewed leaders, who generously shared their stories, some of whom are referred to across the chapters. Insight about leadership clearly goes beyond school leaders. However, I started my research with high school principals because they are in the 'people business' and are encouraged to seek continuous leadership development and invest in building other leaders around them. Additionally, I wanted to observe leadership in practice when the leader can't use positional authority to the degree a military leader can and hasn't a set of handcuffs in their back pocket to make people do what they want. In other words, leaders in schools have to use their personal influence and can't always rely on their positional power to change behaviour.

Educational leaders don't sell products. They are not driven by financial gain. They grow people. They grow potential and hope, not product and profit. To grow people requires substantial influence. It is the people work that is the hardest, in comparison to the other aspects of leadership work, such as managing finance, sales and facilities, developing products and curriculum, training and reporting. School leadership is significantly challenging to get right, as schools are places of uncertainty, ambiguity and complexity, with many layers of leadership. They are an excellent training ground for leadership influence.

Personal connection with the topic

My story began in school. I experienced first-hand the impact and influence of different school leadership approaches in my early days as a middle leader in high schools.

I have poignant memories of observing two particular school leaders in a large city school as they interacted with their team in their role as principal. The deep interest and curiosity I have for this research topic was born out of the social dynamics I observed as I followed these two (seemingly) similar leaders, whose impacts on the motivation and inspiration levels of their teams were dramatically different, leading to significantly contrasting results.

Rod and Mark (not their real names) were both experienced senior high school principals, of similar age and academic backgrounds. They both had a strong work ethic and were considered intelligent men by their peers. Each was kind to me and taught me much about leadership. However, they had very different stories. Our *story* is what others say about us when we are not in the room and represents how others perceive us. Leaders are constantly judged and watched by their teams and a narrative quickly evolves as a result of their behaviours, their perceived intent, the decisions they make, and how they make others feel. The conversation that transpires during an interaction has a lasting impact on how we feel and can make or break the relationship (Scott, 2010). Our story tends to follow us, sometimes uninvited, to job interviews, and sits beside us at meetings. We are known by our story, by reputation, seen through other people's eyes. Despite both principals having served just over two years in the principal role, consecutively, in the same school, Rod and Mark left the school with narratives worlds apart regarding the strength of their inspirational footprint.

Rod had a calm confidence and was held in high esteem, and the team was in awe of the way he led and interacted with others. They loved working for him and would do anything he asked. He had the capacity to build trust and inspire staff, which over time raised staff morale and united a strong team effort. The high-performance learning culture he established as a result raised school results. Rod was promoted, interstate, after only a couple of years at the school.

Mark was generally disliked; some avoided him, others didn't trust him, and as a result, he attracted minimal cooperation. He appeared to dishearten staff and breed confusion and defensiveness, leading to passive resistance, and sometimes active resistance, over time. Mark's words often divided his team and fragmented loyalties and in-fighting soon prevailed. Everyone seemed to have their own agenda, and as a result, academic success was difficult to attain amidst the power struggles. After attracting a critical mass of staff complaints to Central Office, he was transferred and given alternative duties in another area.

During this time, in my role as deputy principal, I worked alongside both men, which provided me with a front-row seat as events unfolded. A deputy principal in a large high school has to be able to step in and out of the principal's role as required. Therefore, I was included in most critical conversations and planning meetings in order to keep up to date, as a normal part of my duties.

Although at the time I could not pinpoint why the two principals' stories were so different, I learnt that year through what other staff said that although we can't control what others think of us, we can influence how others think about us through our social interactions and how we make others feel. Staff opinions of Mark and Rod as leaders seemed to have very little to do with how smart each principal was, the time they had invested in the job, or how many qualifications they had. I wondered, then, what magic Rod possessed that Mark did not. I wanted to figure out why Rod could inspire, unite and deliver, while Mark could incite, divide and derail.

These events formed a watershed moment and learning opportunity in leadership. At this time, I had completed a Bachelor of Education and a Master of Learning Management with a school leadership focus, so I felt my next step should be to study for a psychology degree, hoping it would shed light on human behaviour, which in turn introduced me to the fascinating insights from neuroscience. This led to a transdisciplinary approach to my PhD, the nature of which emerged from my desire to understand what transpires in the space between a high school principal's interactions with his or her team members; to capture what would at first appear as an invisible dynamic of influence in the form of inspiration. I wondered what crucial attributes of a principal's leadership can inspire a team to engage and cooperate – or not.

The leaders I work with today inspire me on a daily basis. As a consultant, I work with principals across private and state schools, military officers, university professors, directors, police, public servants, and corporate chiefs across the map. My brief is to walk alongside these leaders to bolster their influence and their ability to motivate their professional teams to engage, for best performance, success and wellbeing. As I work with them, I aim to communicate their leadership potential so clearly that they are inspired to see it in themselves (Covey, 2006).

To that end, through this research, I have captured a bit of Rod's magic in order to clarify the 'what' through the 12 leadership attributes to build trust, establish rapport and promote growth, the 'how' through the influential strategies, and the 'why' through the neuroscience lens.

Everyone can be a leader

The mission of leaders today is to build other leaders around them, not followers, because you can't build a high-performance learning culture and execute alone. It is about multiplying impact through the development of others. Leading in isolation is not enough to build flourishing schools. The good news is that everyone can be a leader, but they need to see themselves as a leader and know how to define and enact leadership.

Being a leader is about influence and is not reliant on a position of authority or a badge. Neighbours, parents, teachers, students and colleagues can lead. This book will assist with building leaders in schools or wherever you are making a positive difference. The concept of leadership through influence goes beyond schools. Good leadership is good leadership anywhere.

Takeaways

- Leadership is about influence.
- We judge others by their trustworthiness, warmth and credibility.
- Leadership is about doing.
- The brain runs on primitive software, and this has implications for leadership and behaviour.
- The brain was designed to move, connect and problem-solve, yet we live in a world of convenience, isolation and comfort.
- The brain is neuroplastic and changes form in response to our experiences and learning to prepare us for the future.
- Expertise is hardwired from a mix of academic study and lived experience over time. You can't be an instant expert.
- We have neurons in our gut, heart and brain.
- Leaders are made, not born. Everyone can be a leader.
- Leading alone is not enough to build thriving schools.

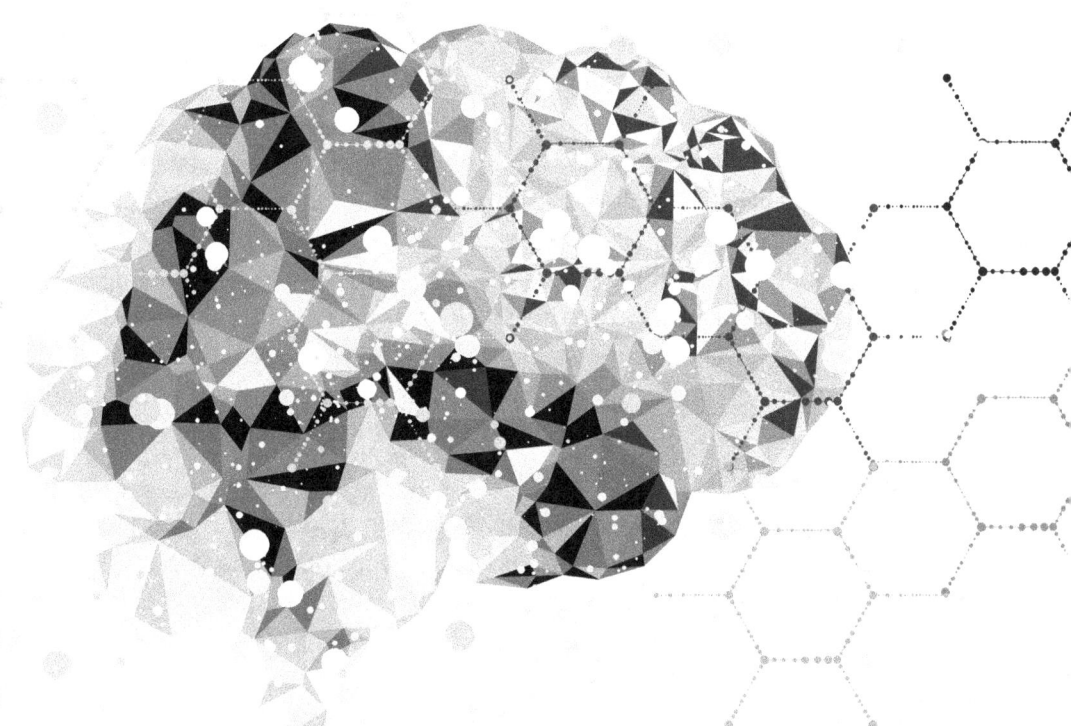

Part 1
Leadership and the Science

'Inspiring people comes down to keying into neurological and psychological triggers in all of us.'

CLAUDIO FESER

Leaders are made not born. However, we are all born with certain hardwired traits, so individuals have different starting points. With experience and learning, these traits are either amplified or minimised. Occasionally, we meet someone who is charismatic and has been gifted with certain traits that tend to attract others and additionally is hardwired with strong specific skill sets. However, most of us need to start with what we have and have quite a bit of work to do to grow into leadership. Therefore, a leader today needs to be highly self-aware to understand their edges (areas of development) and their strengths. If we are not aware of our edges, we don't know how our behaviours and interpersonals (facial expressions and posture) impact on others, and we are unaware of our starting point.

There are three factors that contribute to the likelihood of our ability to strengthen our self-awareness around leadership: our traits (what we are born with), our experience that builds our values, beliefs and skills (things we learn), and our willingness to change, adapt and grow (our mindset and attitude). The first step is to identify your personal starting point and have a clear view about where you want to be and who you want to be. Who you are is how you lead.

The role of emotion in leadership

> *'Great leaders move us. They ignite our passion and inspire the best in us. When we try to explain why they are so effective, we speak of strategy, vision or powerful ideas. But the reality is much more primal. Great leadership works through the emotions...'*
>
> Daniel Coleman

During the advanced stages of my mother's dementia, while she was in a nursing home, I came to a profound realisation: our capacity to feel endures, even as the brain deteriorates. As the disease impaired her prefrontal cortex, the deeper, more primitive regions of her brain, those responsible for emotion, began to govern her thoughts. This shift was unmistakably reflected in the things she said.

She first lost her short-term memory; it was shortened to about ten minutes due to the reduced capacity of the hippocampus. Not long after, she struggled to find the right words to express herself or make a complete sentence, as her temporal lobes were impaired. She talked in a 'fruit salad', as the nurses called it. She would say that the trees were angry, expressing that it was windy. This was a deterioration of the Broca area in her brain, a condition called Broca's aphasia. The phone would ring and she would go to the refrigerator to answer it, as she experienced the loss of the object and facial recognition capacity in her visual cortex. She remembered me, but her memory and recognition of her friendship group was fading fast.

However, one day, with immense effort, she managed to form a coherent sentence. I could see in her face, drawn with concentration, that it meant everything to her. She said, 'I'm sorry you have a mad mother. I can't do anything anymore. But I can feel, and I know I love you.' That moment is etched in my memory. Our capacity to feel can transcend even the sharpest decline of reason. Emotion, in its raw and powerful form, can break through the barriers of illness, hardship and silence – especially the love a mother holds for her child. It is not logic, but the way we feel, that truly endures. Emotion is a game changer.

> *'I've learned that people will forget what you said, people will forget what you did, but people will never forget how you made them feel.'*
> Dr Maya Angelou

Gordon (2022) explains that our emotions were our first language, and there is general agreement that there are six universal emotions. As we interact with one another, emotions emerge, within a fifth of a second, as a nonconscious neurological process (Gordon, 2022), in response to social cues (triggers, tone, words, interpersonals). The tone of our voice has a significant impact (Gordon, 2022) in how we are perceived and read. If the emotion is fear, then we will feel a level of stress at this point and go into a flight-or-fight response. Emotion sets off our physiological response, affecting our heart rate and pupil dilation.

Emotions are associated with our cognitive bias, which is informed by our past experiences. Cognitive bias is a systematic nonconscious error in thinking that leads an individual to misinterpret or distort information. It is a way the brain reserves fuel and is essentially a shortcut (referred to as heuristics) in thinking or a pattern of thinking that is clumped together, based on existing neural networks, associated with our values and beliefs.

Our beliefs influence what is selected from a conversation, and we use this portion of the information to make assumptions and draw conclusions. A feeling follows, which is the psychological response within half a second (Kennedy, 2021), creating our mental state such as defensive or inspired. If we are feeling stressed, we are more likely to agitate rather than contribute, as our behaviours are protective. Alternatively, if we are feeling inspired, we are more likely to contribute and engage.

Thus, our mental state informs our decisions which drive our behaviour. Repeated collective behaviours become habits that create the culture of a workplace. A workplace culture is simply a collection of mindsets and behaviours; the way we do things around here. The work culture can either speed up or slow down the change we want to achieve. If principals are to change behaviour to unite teams towards a common purpose, they need to address emotion as an underlying part of what it is to be human. The thought process outlined above is shown below in Figure 1.

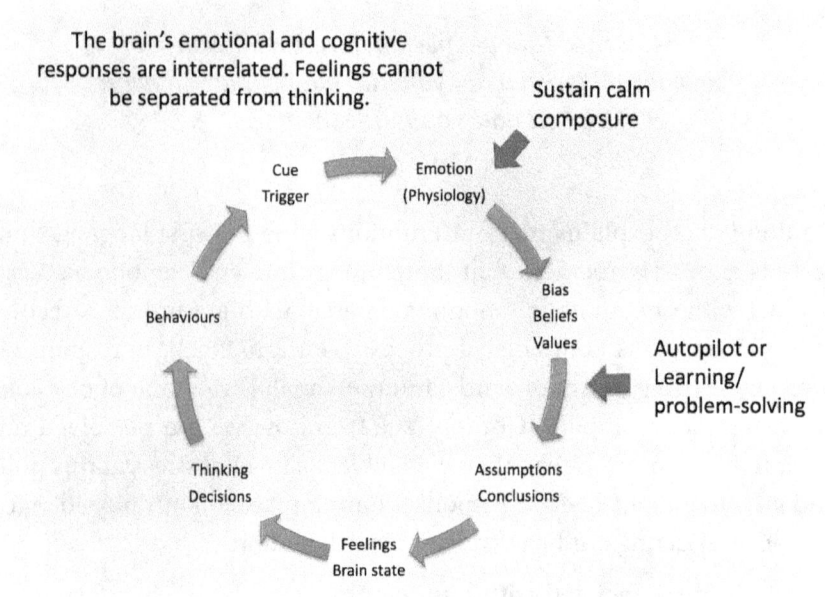

Figure 1: The brain's response during a personal interaction

> 'We are not thinking creatures who feel.
> We are feeling creatures who think.'
> Dr Jill Bolte Taylor

A leader who is tempted to dismiss emotion, the way people feel, when managing problems, will often risk missing the root cause. An influential leader attends to all the layers shown in Figure 1. It is not surprising that what happens in the personal interaction space is mysterious, as much of what occurs is nonconscious and happens in a split second. Studies suggest that the firing of the limbic system aroused by a nonconscious emotion occurs within 8 milliseconds and shows in the face first, taking 40 milliseconds for the information to appear in the neocortex for processing as a conscious cognition in the form of a decision (Kennedy, 2021). Even with the variance in times that different studies show, we can conclude that the human response happens in a split second without our conscious awareness.

During a personal interaction, the brain either invests energy to pay attention to solve a problem or learn something (which takes a lot of fuel) or the brain operates on automatic pilot and relies on heuristics, saving fuel. Thus, a leader needs to be actively present in a social interaction, otherwise their automatic pilot may not serve them well. Paying attention is a skill that can be improved with practice.

Our brain is operating on primitive software

As stated in the introduction, we judge someone in the first few minutes by their trustworthiness, warmth and credibility. Specifically, we ask nonconsciously, 'Can I trust them and am I safe? Do I detect strength? What have I got to lose? Are they open or closed? Can they inspire us?' These questions are related to the brain's primitive and primal role of keeping us safe and are anchored into the importance of trust, aligning to our emotional brain. Indeed, physical and psychological safety is the brain's first and foremost role. A lack of safety will reduce the potential to inspire.

We ask, 'Can I detect strength?' because humans are attracted to strength, as this makes us feel safe, and people draw confidence from a strong leader. 'Are they open or closed?' refers to how safe people feel revealing their vulnerability or their private thoughts and whether they are going to be open and let us in to show their authentic self. All of these responses are about safety and conjure up anxiety and defensive/protective behaviours as a natural human response.

When the trust need is satisfied we look to connection, and we ask ourselves, 'Do I feel a warm connection of acceptance? Are they from my tribe? Do I feel valued and understood? Am I in or out? Can they unite us?' These questions are inherently linked to seeking belonging and aligned to our social brain. We are attracted to people who are like-minded and who like us. This is more about their standard of conduct than their cultural background. When you are repelled by someone, usually you are perceiving something distasteful about their way of being or in their manner or their vibe. For example, they may be too pushy, too brash, too familiar, too cocky, or not using filters (over-sharing). When we ask, 'Are we out or in', we are referring to the inner circle. Without connection, we reduce the potential to unite.

When the trust and rapport needs are both met, we look to credibility and ask ourselves, 'Are they competent? Are they a rational thinker and open to learning? What will I gain? Am I ahead or behind? Can they deliver?' These questions are aligned to our thinking brain and our instinctive drive to learn and move forward. Gaining something is about assessing if the leader is going to be a good mentor and whether I will learn from them. 'Am I ahead or behind?' is referring to whether I will move forward or backward in regard to advancement and getting what I want. The credibility gap is the distance between what they say they can do and what the truth is. Without credibility, we reduce the potential to deliver.

The questions are shown in Table 1.

In summary, this instinctive thinking directly relates to the nature of our emotional, our social and our thinking neural networks. The brain's neural circuits are interrelated, which helps to explain why social interactions between a leader and a team member are highly socially sensitive. Let's take a deeper dive into the three brains.

Vibe we feel	Our thinking
Trustworthiness	• Can I trust them and am I safe? • Do I detect strength? • What have I got to lose? • Are they open or closed? • Can they inspire us?
Warmth	• Do I feel a warm connection of acceptance? • Are they from my tribe? • Do I feel valued and understood? • Am I in or out? • Can they unite us?
Credibility	• Are they competent? • Are they a rational thinker and open to learning? • What will I gain from them? • Am I ahead or behind? • Can they deliver?

Table 1: The three things we judge someone by

Heart, head and gut leadership

The very complex organ of the brain can be represented by a simple metaphor to aid our understanding:

- Brain one (emotional brain)
- Brain two (social brain)
- Brain three (thinking brain).

Brain one, our emotional brain, is hardwired to detect threat. Our emotional brain is linked to the brain stem (breathing) and midbrain (movement) area. This is associated with leadership that is *intuitive*, where our gut feeling rules our instinctive emotional responses. Neuroscientists have found neurons in the gut, some of which operate independently of the brain. Combined neural pathways are hyper-alert to stress and trigger rapid survival responses when we feel unsafe. They are associated with protection and managing threats. The brain nonconsciously checks for threat four or five times a second and has four or five times as many neural networks for negative emotion as positive emotion (Gordon, 2020). Negative emotion is longer lasting and more common than positive emotion, so the brain is said to tip to the negative (Gordon, 2022).

A friend of mine shared a simple story that perfectly illustrates how our brains latch on to negative experiences. He bought a jar of olives for $2.80 from his regular supermarket. When he opened it at home, he realised it was only half full. So, he immediately took it back to the store. Despite being a loyal customer for years, his explanation was met with suspicion. He had to repeat his story to the manager, who finally and reluctantly agreed to provide a refund. That one moment of doubt, of questioning his integrity, erased years of positive shopping experiences at that store. He never went back. He told his friends, who told their friends. The store may have attempted to save $2.80 that day, but it lost far more in the long run. One sour moment can outweigh a hundred good ones. The brain tips to the negative.

If the brain detects threat, our behaviour tends to defend our ground and go into avoid mode, and we are more likely to respond in an 'agitate state'. If the brain does not detect threat and we see something we want or we like, we are more likely to approach and experience a 'contribute' state. The implication for leadership is that a leader needs to be able to inspire the trust of others and be worthy of that trust to bring about a collective contribute state. The brain's lower regions' default is distrust, so when we meet someone new we need to earn the trust of that person. For some, this might only require a handshake and eye contact, but for others it might take several months. Influential leaders understand that they need to protect the safety and interests of the humans in their care.

The second brain is the social brain. Our brain evolved to belong to and operate in a social group. Our social brain is linked to the limbic system and governs our heartfelt feelings. Neuroscientists have reported around 100 million neurons in the heart. This is about leadership that is associated with our *compassion*. The limbic system is a collection of parts including the hippocampus, hypothalamus, thalamus and amygdala. These are associated with moments of joy, rest and connection. When the pathways are stimulated, the brain releases oxytocin and serotonin, increasing empathy, pride, and loyalty, strengthening our ability to connect with others. Building relationships goes beyond a desire for a sense of belonging and connectedness to others to being essential for our wellbeing.

Many studies have shown that social connectedness is a human need for our survival. Without strong bonds in the first 1000 days, the brain suffers developmental problems due to severe sensory deprivation, resulting in a reduction in grey and white matter, cortical atrophy, leading to reduced brain volume. The newborn brain has a number of developmentally sensitive windows in order to establish strong connectivity of the prefrontal cortex to other regions of the brain, which requires certain conditions. If a baby is feeling anxious, unsafe or uncomfortable and does not bond to one calm loving adult, the brain's more primitive areas are active, managing the stress rather than prioritising the development of the area for executive function. The importance of connection for the health of our brain and our general wellbeing extends throughout our life.

Building relationships and rapport between team members is therefore essential in establishing high-performance teams. Effective leaders are relatable to the people they are leading and build rapport to galvanise the unity of the tribe. Once people feel they belong to a specific group, they will take a sense of pride in that group expressed as loyalty. Additionally, many studies have found that the quality of the relationships we have with others will directly impact the level of cooperation. Teams with strong group identity have been shown to act to the benefit of the group, even when doing so has personal costs (Brewer & Kramer, 1986; Haslam et al., 2013; Molenberghs et al., 2015). Strong group identity was found to be associated with increased activity in the reward centres of the brain (Hackel et al., 2017) and the release of the brain chemicals dopamine, serotonin and oxytocin associated with the attachment emotions (joy, love, gratitude). Conversely, social pain and perceived unacceptance from the group activate the survival emotions (anger, fear, disgust), releasing cortisol, and activate a different part of the brain in the cingulate cortex area (Eisenberger, 2012).

A lack of social involvement, reported by a study at Brigham Young University (Holt-Lunstad et al., 2015), was shown to be on a par with smoking in shortening the life span. Dr Susan Pinker (2017) agrees and has described social isolation as *the* next public health risk of our time. Human beings crave connection.

Professor Robin Dunbar (1992), through a study involving primates, found a correlation between the size of the neocortex and the number of meaningful relationships that can be maintained. He suggests that this can be applied to humans and stated that as the team grows larger, trust and communication are at risk of decline. He calls this Dunbar's number: 150. This means that you can only build meaningful relationships with a maximum of 150 people. The implication here is that if your school has over 150 people, you will need to build other leaders around you to share the relationship-building role. You can't lead alone. A lack of unity leads to a 'them and us' mindset, dividing loyalties and eroding a common purpose.

The third brain is the thinking brain. Our brain has an innate desire to learn and achieve. The thinking brain is associated with our prefrontal cortex and is about all things logical and analytical. It drives our need to move forward, learn and achieve success. It is associated with leadership that is *rational*. Overall, we have around 86 billion neurons in the brain. The thinking brain is where conscious thinking occurs associated with the executive functions of critical thinking, problem-solving, higher-order thinking, emotional control, empathy, logical thought, planning, prioritising, short-term memory and indeed our personality. These pathways are maximised when we are not stressed, which allows us to make thoughtful and reasoned decisions.

The emotional, social and thinking brain is shown in Figure 2, along with the names of the key parts of the brain that will be referred to in later chapters.

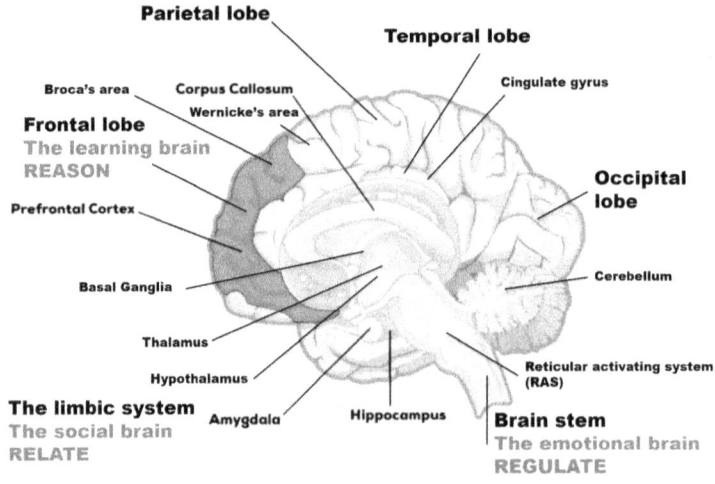

Figure 2 : The brain

> *'Inner strengths are grown mainly from positive states that are turned into positive neural traits.'*
>
> Dr Rick Hanson

Calm, connection, and clarity

If you are wondering about why the metaphor of the three brains is aligned to influence, think about how you feel when you receive shocking negative news, such as the unexpected death of someone you know well. Your heart feels heavy as your social brain feels the loss of the connection. You have a lead knot in your gut as your emotional brain goes into overdrive looking for threat, disrupting your composure, making you feel rattled. You feel numb as your thinking brain's capacity for logical thought is diminished, taking away your clarity. It is not the time to make big decisions. Your whole physiology changes and your mood is affected. You no longer feel calm, connected and clear. This is the three brains at work, because there is a brain–body connection.

We often hear about cognitive load, but humans also experience emotional and sensory load. Cognitive load is associated with the head, emotional load is associated with the heart, and sensory load is linked to the gut. When all three are in full force, we feel rather spent or ill and need to rest and refuel.

The three brains also have an impact on the way we make decisions, because the neural networks are interrelated. The most significant difference is between the lower regions of our brain, being fast and instinctive, and the upper parts of the brain, which are more considered and disciplined. This concept is shown in Table 2.

Table 2 shows what is happening for head, heart and gut leadership. We want leaders who can use their head, heart and gut in their leadership approach to inspire, unite and deliver. The science of leadership is about knowing when to use your head, when to use your heart, and when to use your gut to make the best decision for the context – or when to use all three.

Brain	Thinking and feeling	
The emotional brain - This is *intuitive* leadership or gut leadership. - It's about trust and safety. - It affects our ability to remain calm and inspire. - If overloaded, it can lead to sensory load.	- Reading the room - Spontaneous - Experience - Biased - Prejudiced - Uncontrolled - Automatic - Immediate	- Intuitive - Rigid - Emotional - Instinctive - Fears - Cues - Triggers - Protective - Impressions
The social brain - This is *compassionate* leadership or heart leadership. - It's about rapport and warmth. - It affects our ability to connect to unite. - If overloaded, it can lead to emotional load.	- Hopeful - Empathetic - Feeling - Heartfelt - Connected - Relating - Values - Memories - Dreams	- Friendly - Responsive - Compassion - Kindness - Likeability - Passion - Beauty - Collaborative
The thinking brain - This is *rational* leadership or head leadership. - It's about growth and achievement. - It affects our ability for clarity to deliver. - If overloaded, it can lead to cognitive load.	- Disciplined - Reflective - Mindful - Considered - Critical - Self-regulating - Self-correcting - Self-control - Open to perspectives - Proactive - Reason and logic	- Learning - Analytical - Rational thinking - Challenge assumptions - Truth-seeking - Evidence - Curious - Command and control - Attention

Table 2: Head, heart and gut leadership

Head leadership is about rational, controlled, disciplined leadership and clarity. Leaders who use their head are self-disciplined, can recognise their own limitations, can regulate their own emotional state to remain composed, and are willing to seek feedback. They stay curious and question how things are going. They see other points of view. They make sound decisions based on evidence and logical problem-solving. The thinking brain will serve you well, as it can cut through the noise that sometimes biases your judgment. It is about delivering outcomes. This is brain three at work.

Heart leadership is about care, compassion and the ability to unite. We want leaders who can use their heart, to connect, encourage, and allow others to shine. They know the importance of being able to take their ego out. Heart leadership seeks to understand, shows empathy, and cares about the tribe. It assesses situations through the heart, showing warmth, seeing the beauty and projecting hope to unite the team. This is brain two at work.

Gut leadership is about courage, sensing, intuition and the ability to inspire. We want leaders who can lead through their gut by building their expertise to such a high level that they can read the room. This positions them well to be responsive with intuitive action. They quickly perceive impressions through instinct. When you have a deep lived experience and academic expertise in a specialised field, you notice and feel things that you may not be able to explain. You more easily understand the context through detecting mood, potential and weaknesses as your emotional brain notices cues from the setting. This is helpful for leaders, as they need to be proactive and responsive to understand what is happening and what might happen around the corner to address potential problems. Their gut instinctively gives them a reading, and this is leading through your gut. This is brain one at work.

Intuition can be a powerful ally in decision-making or a potential liability. When I was 17, my father bought me my first car: a classic Mini. I drove that little car well into my thirties. One day, I told my husband that something felt off with the steering. 'What makes you think that?' he asked. I didn't have a clear answer. It was just a very strong feeling I had while driving. Trusting my instincts, he took the car in for a service and mentioned the concern to the mechanics. They inspected it but found nothing wrong. A week later, I was cruising down the highway when the steering was suddenly wrenched out of my hands. I lost control as the car skidded across a bridge. Thankfully, there was no other traffic, and I came to a stop just before crashing into the guardrail on the other side of the road. I tried restarting the car, but it was dead. When it was towed into the workshop, the mechanics discovered that the suspension supports had rusted through and snapped. That moment taught me something profound: intuition isn't magic – it's our brain processing subtle cues based on experience, often before we're consciously aware of them. In this case, my intuition helped me stay alert and cautious, which may have made all the difference. Intuition is about detecting cues from experience, so my brain had subconsciously noticed something beyond what I could logically explain.

Likewise, in the movie *The Bourne Supremacy* (2004), Jason Bourne reveals a moment when gut instinct led to a quick decision removing him from danger. Jason and his girlfriend, Marie Kreutz, are in Goa, India, and are at the marketplace enjoying a quiet stroll. Jason notices subtle signs that they are being watched. His instincts kick in, and he scans the crowd, identifying a stranger who looks suspicious. He tells Marie 'We're blown', although to the viewer there is nothing out of place. Jason acts immediately and leads Marie away. He doesn't stop to check for hard evidence, but as they escape they realise his gut instinct was right. They run for their lives. In this moment, the emotional brain springs into action, checking for threat, picking up cues, instinctive, immediate and actionary.

However, there is a caution for leadership to be considered here. Only experts with decades of lived experience can effectively use their gut in decision-making, and only in their area of expertise. Novices who attempt to use their intuition as the sole factor in decision-making run the risk of making inaccurate assumptions and errors in judgment. Decision-making by the novice requires evidence. This is because the novice brain is different from the expert brain. The expert brain has hardwired many schemas over time that help it make connections for quick decisions. Additionally, leaders who prize themselves as decisive need to be mindful that complex decisions in uncertain contexts require consultation, reflection and analysis over time. Also, when your intuition detects danger, there may not be any. At times leaders need to override the fear they feel and lean into the discomfort and forge ahead to problem-solve, resisting the temptation to avoid or give up or take the easy route. For example, you may have to have a difficult conversation with a resistant person; your gut is telling you to avoid it but your head is reminding you to push on.

Leading with the head, heart and gut

Luci Quinn is a principal of a large secondary college and has a deep lived experience and expertise, reflected in her remarkable ability to lead from the head, heart and gut. On my visits to her school, I noticed that Luci is able to embrace transparency in candid conversations, while maintaining warmth in her communication, showing a consistency of integrity. She appears to have an intuition about what to say when, which puts people at ease. This instinctive response in her ability to read the room is brain one (emotional brain) at work. She is highly loyal and shows compassion when coaching the leaders around her. This is brain two (social brain) at work. She has built a high level of credibility as she acts with confidence in high-pressure situations, focusing on the things that matter. This is brain three (thinking brain) at work.

Some years ago, Luci shared with her leadership team that she recognised the need for a restructure of roles. Many of the members of the leadership team had served in the traditional roles for a significant period of time, one of them as college organiser. It was time to restructure to enable the college culture to align with a new shared vision in order to move forward. She understood that this type of change could raise anxiety and uncertainty, as it is unsettling. While it wasn't anything personal, the human response is to feel defensive and take it personally.

Once the structure was finalised, after a period of consultation, she presented it to the assistant principals. Rather than spilling all the roles and advertising externally, and in that process invalidating their work, she recognised that each of them had demonstrated competency, commitment and credibility, building trust with the community in their previous roles. She felt that it wasn't fair to cast them aside when they had done their job as best they could under the conditions they were in. Instead, she offered them the opportunity to step into a new space and showed that she believed there was capacity for growth. In the wash-up, one chose to retire, one chose the role most aligned to their previous role, and the others were open to change.

The most significant challenge was for the assistant principal (AP), who had been college organiser, as there was nothing in the new structure even remotely like that. This AP had a passion and love for the college, attention to detail, an embodiment of the college ethos and values, and a deep knowledge of the community. When he made his choice of role, he shared his excitement and hesitation. Luci discussed how she would provide support, but also ensured there was clarity of expectations, explaining what she needed to see within the first three years of the contract and the process she would undertake before future contract renewal.

He stepped into the challenge of this new role by leaning into all of his strengths as the assistant principal in community and culture. He embraced new learning by completing a master's in educational leadership, which was a significant commitment on his part, having not studied since his initial degree. Luci noticed this experience was reflected in the way he began to lead. She commented that it certainly wasn't always easy, as he was leading others who perhaps had more content knowledge in the area; however, together they engaged in regular, honest, authentic and robust feedback and dialogue about how things were going, what she was needing from him, and where he was contributing to the success of the leadership team. He was genuinely wanting to be the best he could be. All of this was built on a relationship of trust and a deep belief in the capacity to learn and grow.

Luci watched the AP find his voice and his place in contributing to, challenging, and bringing creativity and ideas to the leadership team. Recently, after a meeting in which she had a robust strategic dialogue, Luci commented, 'I noticed how you shared some great insights today in our conversation. Would you have done that three or four years ago?' His reply was, 'No, because it wasn't what I felt my role was. Back then I just stayed in my lane.' The willingness to grow and be coachable is a leadership strength of an influential leader, and this was clearly shown by the AP through his professionalism. This also illustrates that sometimes we don't provide the opportunity for others to step up their leadership but expect them to see themselves as leaders. Luci created the setting for this to happen. Next month the AP will attend his graduation with his family to receive his master's degree.

This is an example of a principal leading with their head, heart and gut. Luci intuitively understood that the assistant principal had significant potential that had not been tested or tapped into. She judged him by his potential, not his story. This is gut leadership. She led through her heart by showing compassion and loyalty, believing in her colleagues' potential and protecting their best interests. She led through her head, by reshaping her team roles to align with the college vision, despite initial discomfort and challenges. Luci is an exceptional role model of influential leadership.

The lying brain

The lower regions of the brain are sometimes called the honest brain and the upper regions of the brain are sometimes referred to as the lying brain. This is because the thinking brain can lie and the lower brain cannot. When you lie, unless you are a psychopath with inbuilt abnormal responses, the emotional brain will present some 'tells' to give you away. Tells are the nonconscious things that we do to show what we are truly thinking and feeling, despite the words we use. They could include a blink of the eye, an increased heart rate, pupil changes, swirling our hair, touching our nose, or a pacifying action such as rubbing the upper legs when sitting. Certain combinations and the timing of tells can identify when you are telling the truth or lying, or if you are anxious or relaxed.

When I was in the Greek islands, I was crowd-watching and I saw a very short man talking to a tall man. They were standing on a slope near the town square. The short man, little by little, shuffled and manoeuvred himself around during the conversation until he was standing at the high point and the tall man had been quietly nudged to the low point as his personal space had been slowly intruded upon. As the shorter man was talking, he had hold of his cap brim and was moving it up and down on his head to give the impression of added height. These were nonconscious actions that revealed his thinking. He had noticed there was a significant height difference, and for some reason it did not sit well with him, so his body responded at some level.

If leaders don't maximise transparency and avoid hidden agendas, trust will decline. The level of psychological safety you feel and your confidence level, wired by past experience, will determine the degree to which you open your private thoughts and feelings to others (Edmondson, 2019).

If you are too closed as a leader, you run the risk of people not being able to get to know you, and they will fill the gaps with their own assumptions to complete your story. This may impact the degree of influence that you have.

The three brains are integrated and sequential

When we are stressed, we don't have full access to the prefrontal cortex (our thinking brain), and the lower regions of the brain (our emotional brain) are more active. The messages simply don't get through to our logical, reasoning brain and we operate on instinctive emotion. To make rational decisions, we need to be calm and composed (Willis, 2020).

This is because the three brains (emotional, social and thinking) are integrated and sequential at neural level. You can't separate cognition from emotion, which means you can't separate feeling from thinking. This would imply that a leader needs to calm the brain stem to build trust, and tap into the limbic system to build rapport in order to stimulate the prefrontal cortex for learning and growth. This has significant implications for leadership:

1. The way we feel about someone or something will determine our willingness to engage and cooperate at our best.
2. The culture we create as a result of the collective feelings will drive behaviours that will either speed up or slow down the change we want to create.
3. Leaders need to pay attention to their emotional impact as they interact with others and improve their agility around changing mental states at critical times.
4. Leaders need to be able to mitigate their instinctive emotional first response and cognitive bias to maintain a calm composure in order to make rational decisions.
5. Leaders can actively aim to prime conversational chemistry to shift feelings that create positive helpful states.
6. Leaders need to shape their behaviours, words and tone around the attributes that build trust, rapport and growth so that their interactions align with how the brain operates, rather than going against it.

7. Trust and communication decline as the team grows larger if other leaders are not sharing the leadership.
8. Be mindful that your tells may reveal what you are thinking, so honesty and transparency are essential.

Contribute and agitate brain states

As emotion is at the heart of our social interactions, the brain is triggered into two key states, often called the avoid–approach theory. There are numerous studies that support the avoid–approach theory, and it has been well documented that we move towards things we want and away from things we want to avoid as a key premise underpinning behaviour. Earlier psychological studies were built on by the more recent neuroscience studies, and it was Dr Evian Gordon who put the spotlight on the fact that our brain's role is to maximise reward and minimise threat. More recently I built on Gordon's work and refer to the brain domains as *contribution state* and *agitation state*. Table 3 shows the evolution of brain state theory and the associated research and authors.

It is very easy to trigger someone into agitate state, even if your intentions are positive. In a study by Dr Wendy Wood and her colleagues, two groups of people were given a paper maze that featured a mouse. One group had a picture of cheese at the end of the maze and the other group had an owl hunting the mouse. The groups were asked to take the mouse through the maze in order to find the exit. After completing this activity, the groups were given creative problem-solving tests. The group with the cheese outperformed the group with the owl. The results of this study, which have been supported by other similar research, show that the subtle difference in the board made a big impact on the thinking of the participants. The cheese group were in contribute state and had open access to their prefrontal cortex for creative problem-solving. The owl group tended to be in agitate state, increasing activity in their lower brain regions, creating a protective state, reducing their ability to problem-solve. This study underscores how the brain state influences creativity and problem-solving. People tend to be more flexible to overcome challenges if they are not stressed. On the other hand, while in threat mode, their cognitive performance is hindered by anxiety. This highlights the role of emotion in motivation.

Avoidance response	Approach response	Researcher
The Karpman triangle: victim, aggressor, rescuer	Learner, teacher, negotiator	Karpman (1968)
Threat mode: release of cortisol, adrenaline	Reward mode: release of oxytocin, dopamine, serotonin and noradrenaline	Gordon et al. (2008)
Prevention cues	Promotion cues	Friedman & Förster (2001)
Activates the sympathetic nervous system: stressed, flustered and on high alert	Activates the parasympathetic nervous system: calm, comfortable and focused	Sapolsky (2004)
Move away	Move towards	Lieberman (2007)
Threat mode: defensive or resistant	Reward mode: inspired and engaged	Rock (2008)
Thinking narrows	More innovative	Frederickson (2011); Horwitch & Chipple-Callahan (2016); Jung-Beeman et al. (2008)
11 brain regions deactivated including: posterior cingulate cortex (social network); left inferior frontal gyrus (mirror system) 6 regions activated including: bilateral anterior cingulate cortex (narrowing attention); left posterior cingulate cortex (less compassions)	14 regions activated including: anterior cingulate cortex (attention); right inferior frontal gyrus (social network); right inferior parietal lobe (mirror system); right putamen and bilateral insula (relationships)	Boyatzis (2012)
Aversive feelings	Appetitive feelings	Kandel (2012)

Avoidance response	Approach response	Researcher
Emotions inhibit synaptic growth	Emotions build neural architecture	Hanson (2015)
Reflexive brain state, high stress response, flight or fight	Reflective brain state, low stress response, rest and digest	Arsten (2015)
Survival emotions of fear, anger, disgust, distrust, shame and sadness	Attachment emotions of trust, joy, inspiration, hope, gratefulness and curiosity	Swart et al. (2015) Wang (2019)
Limbic response inhibits executive brain	Prefrontal cortex active and accessible; more open to logic and learning	Willis (2016)
Stress state: heart rate increases, blood pressure rises, inflammation, muscles tight, sweating, fast breaths, gut inactive, pupils dilate	Relaxed state: pupils constrict, flexible, slow breaths, gut active, muscles relaxed, feeling of satisfaction.	Gordon (2022)
Inhibition system: scarcity, defensive, rigidity, threat, inaction	Approach system: abundance, secure, cognitively agile, opportunities, action	Cuddy (2022)
Agitate state: defensive, resistant, protective Untrustworthy, lacking warmth and lacking credibility	Contribute state: inspired, engaged, cooperative Trustworthy, warmth and credibility	Newman (2022)
Incoherence shows change in heart rate (HRV) when feeling negative emotions such as frustration, anger and impatience	Coherence shows change in heart rate (HRV) when feeling positive emotions such as joy, contentment and gratitude	McCraty & Shaffer (2023)

Table 3: The evolution of brain states

The social influence model (SIM)

Figure 3 shows the underpinning conceptual framework that informed recent research (Newman, 2022) in Australian high schools that explored how principals inspire their teams to engage in the improvement agenda of the school. It shows why emotion has a central role and influence in human interaction, indicating why it is so challenging for a leader to motivate others to bring about change. However, it also provides hope in that it shows that if they understand the neuroscience, leaders will know how to adjust their behaviour to align with the physiology rather than going against it, becoming more inspirational as leaders.

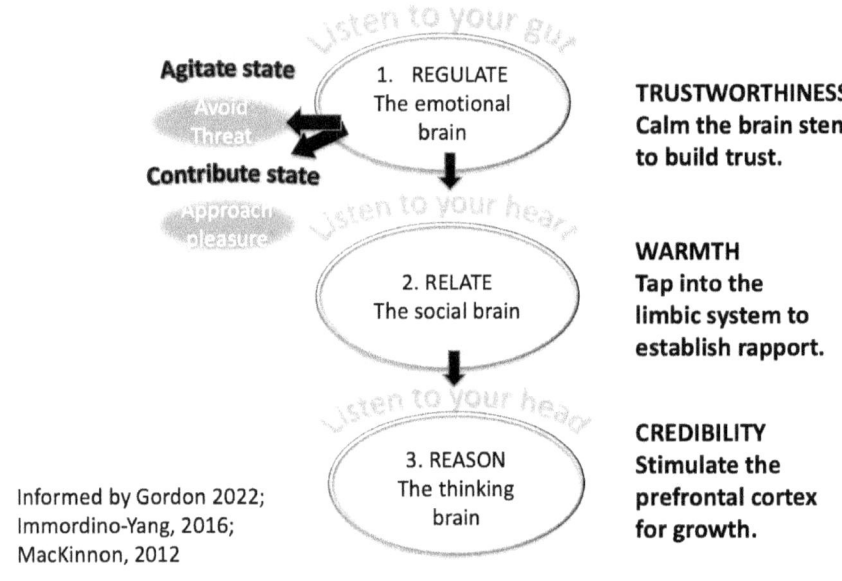

Figure 3: The social influence model (Newman, 2022)

*'Using [brain] knowledge allows leaders to
better understand the brain to align their behaviour
with the physiology, not against it.'*
Yinying Wang (2019)

The power of trust

The building of trust is the essential core business of every leader across the areas of sport, schools, churches, politics, business and voluntary organisations. 'Once trust becomes part of the culture, it works to liberate people to do their best, to give others their best' (Browning, 2020, p.15). Many studies have shown that trust is central to successful leadership, but trust is tricky to build and sustain in the workplace. Covey (2006) maintains that if the leader does not trust the person they are interacting with, the team member will pick up on subtle cues through mirror neurons and reflect that distrust back.

Distrust is associated with increased activity in the insular cortex and amygdala being detected when we experience negative emotions of disgust and fear such as being stigmatised by others (Dimoka, 2010; Wicker et al., 2003). Trust is associated with increased activity in the ventral tegmental area and caudate nucleus, the release of oxytocin when anticipating positive rewards, and the assessment of fairness (Dimoka, 2010; Kruger et al., 2007; Schaufenbuel, 2014). The brain detects trust within milliseconds of meeting someone. The default of the limbic system is to first distrust until the brain has collected more information to update the impression. The brain takes in the person's appearance, tone of voice, gestures and what is said. The implication for leadership is that trust needs to be earned and the leader needs to be worthy of that trust. There are significant and numerous studies that support that trust is the cornerstone of inspirational leadership and essential for bringing out the best performance and engagement in workers (Covey, 2006).

Relational leadership

Building trust goes hand in hand with forming positive relationships. Decades of research into effective leadership practice have culminated in several paradigms of relational leadership theory, including transformational, charismatic, servant, neuroleadership and inspirational leadership, all of which have been identified as effective models for school leadership.

Avolio et al. (2009), Balthazard et al. (2012), Feser (2016) and Sergiovanni (2004), show that these styles are inherently human in their approach and dependent on the leader being highly self-aware and tuned into other people's needs, and are concerned with follower behaviour and motivations (Bass & Bass, 2009). There is general agreement that leadership influence is more effective if teams are inspired by their leaders rather than coerced into action. Haslam and Platow (2001) concluded that leaders who focus on the group (rather than themselves) connect with others to create a shared identity and are the most capable of inspiring followers. More recently, social identity theory focuses on relationships, making salient the role of followers as a key part of leadership, the leader making personal sacrifices for the team and the leader engaged in the 'we' and 'us' language rather than 'I' and 'me' language (Haslam et al., 2013).

A leader's behaviour during a personal interaction can strengthen or weaken a group's social identity. Numerous studies demonstrate that the language a leader uses can either inspire or undermine group loyalties. In one such study by Haslam et al. (2013), the speeches of prime ministers were examined from 1901 to 2013, with the findings indicating that the prime ministers who used 'us' and 'we' language rather than 'I' and 'me' language in their speeches won the election 80 per cent of the time. School principals can also be strategic about how they use words to this end.

Another way a leader can connect to others is through their 'emotional wake' (Scott, 2010) – what we leave after our social interaction with someone (essentially the feeling we leave them with). When a leader is engaged in a conversation with a team member, they will unconsciously give off warmth or not (Fiske et al., 2002). To radiate warmth, leaders need to be composed.

Wellbeing and brain states

Maintaining composure is also important to our wellbeing as leaders. When we are continually stressed, we not only are in a poor position to make logical decisions, but our brain is also releasing cortisol (and adrenaline), which if allowed to continually build up can make us ill. Cortisol has a role in that it prepares us to deal with a stressful event, but sometimes our brain gets tricked into a habitual stress response even when there is no real threat.

The two general states of agitate and contribute can be divided into six 'channels'. It is an important skill for a leader to be able to change brain states at critical times to maintain their composure for their own wellbeing and also to be able to tap into cognitive functionality. Later in the book, we explore ways a leader can self-regulate their brain state. For now, we discuss the six brain states I call channels.

The channels are a metaphor to help our understanding of a complex process which incorporates brainwave variation and neurofeedback (Wang & Hsieh, 2013). They are associated with a small area of the brain called the locus coeruleus (LC). The locus coeruleus appears as a tiny blue stain in the brain stem at ear level, and has around 50,000 neurons (Storoni, 2024). It produces a neurotransmitter called noradrenaline which affects arousal, regulating our focus and alertness. The more noradrenaline released, the higher our arousal.

This chemical response in our brain is connected to physical clues in our body, including changes in the pupils and heart-rate patterns (Storoni, 2023). The more active the LC, the wider the eyes dilate. The pupil dilation can be a give-away, 'a tell', to indicate the level of heightened arousal. For example, if a man looks at a women he is very attracted to, you might see a flicker of the eye pupil showing a clear physiological response, even though the man does not have any conscious control over this change. Dr Rollin McCraty, Director of Research of the Heartmath Institute in California, believes that heart rate variability (HRV) has a 75 per cent accuracy rate in indicating brain state emotions. HRV is the natural variation in time between heartbeats, which is usually measured in milliseconds, and a healthy heart has complex oscillations. The key point here is that our physiology, how we feel, directly responds to our brain state. How we feel impacts our performance and wellbeing.

Control your remote control

The LC is associated with our ability to switch to different brain states so it is helpful to learn how to change channels from anxious and emotional to calm and confident. A school leader navigates a range of scenarios throughout the day that build his or her cognitive, sensory and emotional load, raising stress levels. Being able to change your brain state at critical times is essential for your wellbeing and composure. Imagine you have a remote control for your brain and you can switch channels to bring about a state that is optimal for your purpose or context. Sometimes we need to channel up and sometimes we need to channel down. For example, if we are stressed and carrying a high cognitive load, we need to channel down. If we are sluggish and sleepy, we need to build our cognitive load and channel up. Table 4 outlines the channels.

Channel	Brain state	What is happening
1	Sleep	**Nil arousal–nil focus:** We need to sleep for brain wellness and to consolidate memory.
2	Autopilot	**Low arousal–low focus:** This is when you are feeling sluggish because you have just woken up or you are tired and are not thinking clearly but feel like you are running on automatic. You may be bored and experiencing brain fog. In this state you have low focus and low cognitive load. You don't want to be on this channel when you are rock climbing.
3	Insightful	**Medium arousal–wandering focus:** This is a nice feeling of contentment and your mind is wandering but in a trance-like state. This state is conducive to creativity, innovation and emerging 'aha' moments. This is a dream-like, zombie-like, inward-thinking state. You are not focusing on the issue. You are often in this state when walking on the beach, in the shower, at 2pm in the morning after a deep sleep or doing the mowing. It is when those ideas or solutions come to you out of nowhere.
4	Present	**High arousal–high focus:** In this state you feel sharp and attentive and have clarity of thought. You have full access to the prefrontal cortex, so it is the ideal condition for learning and higher-order thinking. You have your wits about you and you are fully present in conversations with others.
5	Flow	**High arousal–intense focus:** You are so focused that you are absorbed in the task and lose all sense of time. You don't hear outside noise, and the challenge of the task matches your level of expertise. You are not aware of the brain state until you are interrupted. This brain states opens the opportunity for your expertise to flow. This is the ideal channel for painting or studying.
6	Overload	**Too much arousal–focus distracted:** This is a stressful state where there is too much noise for your brain to manage. The lower regions of the brain dominate, and your physiology responds to prepare for flight or flight. Access to the prefrontal cortex is diminished, so your logical decision-making is not at its best. You are on cognitive overload and you feel wired and hypervigilant and may experience brain block.

Table 4: Take control of your remote control

Figure 4 Illustrates the remote control metaphor showing the different channels.

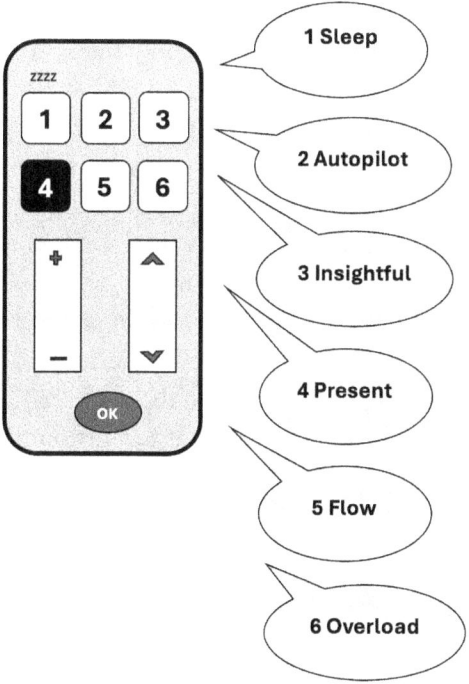

Figure 4: Take control of your internal remote control

How do you switch channels?

An essential leadership skill for today's workplace is the ability to change brain states at critical times. For learning, conversation and problem-solving, you want to be in channel 3, 4 or 5, depending on the purpose and context. To move from channel 2 to 4 (from autopilot to present), you need to increase your cognitive load or arousal level. Your brain activity is affected by your body activity because there is a mind–body connection. If you are feeling sluggish, go for a brisk walk, or if you are sitting in a boring meeting where you want to poke your eye out with a pen (just joking), start some doodling on your notepad or take notes. Waiting to be motivated while you are on autopilot may not work. Doing, in itself, is very motivating. One strategy is to tell yourself, 'If I just do the task for one hour, I can then reward myself with reading my book.'

Multi-tasking has had a bad rap (and so it should) as the brain uses much less fuel when we single-task. When we think we are multi-tasking, our brain is actually moving from one task to the other and uses a lot of fuel building the cognitive load. When you multi-task, you may also miss something important, as your brain can only think about one thing at a time unless you have the other task very much hardwired. For example, you can talk to someone while you tie your shoelaces because your lacing technique is hardwired and automatic. However, when in channel 2, increasing your cognitive load by multi-tasking will help you channel up. For example, designing a concept map while notetaking at a meeting or listening to a podcast and taking notes might be exactly what you need at the time. Moving from 6 to 4 (from overload to present) needs the opposite action, because you need to slow the mind down. You can do this by slowing the body response through box breathing, sitting in the garden bird-watching, or taking a moment to still your thinking.

As the brain tips to the negative, leaders need strategies so they don't get hijacked by their instinctive emotional responses. It is a matter of finding ways that work for you to help retain and sustain your calm composure. Know your triggers, strengths and thresholds (Gordon, 2022). Table 5 outlines a number of strategies leaders can use to calm their brain state.

Technique	Information
Box breathing	Take a deep breath for a count of 4 and hold it for 4 seconds. Let it out for 4 seconds and hold for 4 seconds. Repeat two more times.
Posturing	Hold your posture in a winning confident pose for 15 seconds (like Superman or Superwoman). When we win, we expand our body posture. When we lose, we make ourselves smaller, and when we feel powerless, we want to hide (Cuddy, 2022). Expanded body posture stimulates brain chemicals that can boost our confidence.
Music	Listen to uplifting music for 2 minutes.
Laughter	Find something or someone that is funny. Just the act of smiling can change your brain chemistry.

Technique	Information
Gratitude	Pause. Think of three things you are grateful for. Gratitude is linked to feeling significant. The way you feel will impact your body's physiological response.
Mindfulness	Be aware of how you are feeling and what thoughts come to mind. Name the emotion. Once named, you are more likely to be able to let the emotion go.
Reframe	Reframe your perspective with a growth mindset. Be solution-focused not problem-based. Be future-focused not stuck in the past. If your football team is losing, think how lucky you are to be at the game.
Slow down	Slow down your thinking. Pause. Think about your thinking. Ask questions. Don't make assumptions.
Switch channels	When uninvited thoughts flood in, cut the thought process off and think of something nice. Go to your calm place in your mind.
Change the environment	Go somewhere else.
Self-distancing	Give yourself advice, then go somewhere in a time machine. What would this mean in five years' time?
Compartmentalise	Give yourself permission to only think about it at certain times.
Lean in	Lean into anger or frustration to do better. Prove them wrong.
Imagery and focus	If you are feeling brain fog, imagine diving into cold deep water. If you have too much traffic in your head, slow down and imagine soaking in a warm bubble bath.
Movement	Go for a walk in the wild. Experience the calming effect of the soft curves of nature and move away from the sharp lines of the cityscape.
Brain break	When on cognitive overload, take a brain break. A brain break is anything that is joyful that does not involve new learning and is about 2–10 minutes long, depending on the level of cognitive load you are shifting.

Table 5: Ways to change mind state

Regulating emotions

A longitudinal study by Richmond-Rakerd et al. (2021) studied 1000 babies over the first half of their life span. They reported that children who struggle to regulate their emotions:

- Do worse at school
- Are four times more likely to be convicted of a crime
- Are at greater risk of substance abuse
- Reported poorer-quality relationships
- Reported higher levels of anger, depression and loneliness, and
- Struggle with uncertainty.

By the age of 32, they had lower levels of emotional regulation and higher risks of struggling financially. By 45, the effects were visible in 19 biological aging markers such as blood pressure, white cell count, lung capacity, tooth decay and cholesterol levels.

If you can change your thinking about a situation, you can change how you feel, and this will have an impact on your physiology as the brain is linked to the body. High self-control in early life is associated with slower aging and better preparedness for the later challenges in life.

The wellness cab

The wellness cab framework represents a simple summary of a literature review. It is not rocket science; rather it is about focusing on some good old-fashioned basics to look after the brain. There are many studies to support the benefits of exercise, nutrition and quality sleep for brain wellness. Aging is about wellness, not the number of years. To be in a position to serve others, leaders need to take care of themselves first. The wellness cab components are listed in Table 6.

Now that we have explored the foundations of applied neuroscience for social interactions, the next section looks to the research carried out in schools to identify how principals inspire teams to draw out their best performance.

W	Wilderness and wellbeing habits	Our brain relaxes in the soft curves of the natural bush away from noise, pollution and the sharp angles of the city. Create good wellness habits.
E	Exercise	We have been designed to keep moving.
L	Learning and stimulating novel experiences	Take on challenging learning and strengthen your neural networks with new, exciting experiences.
L	Love, friendship and joy	Invest in connecting with others. Find the joy in your life and lean into it.
N	Nutrition and water	Eat fresh, non-processed foods for brain, gut and heart health. Keep hydrated.
E	Elicit professional help when required	Seek help for physical and mental problems and have proactive check-ups.
S	Self-talk	Check your self-talk for automatic negative thinking patterns. Adopt a helpful mantra.
S	Sleep and stillness	Quality sleep for brain repair, recovery and memory consolidation. Find some stillness.
C	Calming techniques	Practise de-stressing techniques and emotional regulation.
A	Abstain from drugs and smoking	Avoid harmful drugs.
B	Breathing techniques	Be mindful of how you are breathing to ensure you are taking in enough oxygen.

Table 6: The wellness cab

The research in schools

In my research, as mentioned at the beginning of the book, I followed high-performing secondary principals and recorded everything they said and did. I then asked them how they inspired, motivated and influenced their teams to draw out their best performance. I also interviewed their staff and asked, 'How does a leader inspire you to perform at your best?'

As I analysed the data, three very exciting findings emerged. First, the data could be divided into 12 leadership attributes with only one outlier.

Saturation point was reached quite early with all 12 attributes emerging from each school's data, meaning that as I interviewed more staff, the data was very similar, with no new findings after two-thirds of the interviews.

Second, the 12 attributes could be grouped into three clear categories, each associated with the three neural networks of emotional, social and thinking brains. This correlation showed that a third of the attributes were aligned with inspiring trust, a third helped establish rapport, and a third were associated with growth. This implied that an understanding of the brain in regard to applied neuroscience could shed light on why these attributes were effective behaviours for influential leaders. The attributes associated with trust aligned with the emotional brain neural networks, the attributes associated with rapport aligned with the social brain neural networks, and the attributes associated with growth aligned with the thinking brain neural networks.

Third, the different schools had similar findings even though they were located in different areas and were a mix of country and city schools. The shape of the spider graphs showed the data was very similar, suggesting that school staff have a common view about what good school leadership feels like and looks like. Table 7 shows examples of what school staff and principals said when interviewed about the research question and identifies the 12 attributes that align with each comment. The key interview question was: 'What does a principal do or say to inspire you to perform at your best performance?'

What they said

These findings informed my reflections on what effective leadership in schools looks like and how it might be defined.

Attribute	Quote
Strength	<ul><li>'The hard issues are dealt with and not swept under the carpet.'</li><li>'He has a strong positional voice.'</li><li>'I can be very loyal to a leader if I can see their competence and wisdom.'</li><li>'He had the hard conversations.'</li><li>'He was confident and composed.'</li></ul>

Attribute	Quote
Integrity	- 'He had credibility.' - 'She has clear boundaries.' - 'There were no back-door conversations.' - 'He led people in a way that reflects what he wanted from them.' - 'She was fair.'
Humility	- 'He makes me feel like we are on an even playing field.' - 'He is very human… he has humility.' - 'She is approachable.' - 'He could take his ego out.'
Clarity	- 'I am clear about my role.' - 'He brought clarity into chaos.' - 'He was consistent.'
Positivity	- 'She is enthusiastic and hopeful.' - 'He kept most things positive.' - 'If people are happy, productivity will skyrocket.' - 'She could spot potential in people.' - 'She has a strong, positive vibe and energy.' - 'He could speak with passion.' - 'She continually improved and innovated.'
Connectedness	- 'He had our back.' - 'He built strong relationships and rapport.' - 'He took me on as a human first.' - 'She was interested in me as a person first.' - 'He was encouraging in nature.' - 'He got to know me beyond my role.'
Appreciation	- 'He wrote handwritten postcards.' - 'She says thank you, acknowledges and praises.' - 'She notices not just what I do but how I do it.' - 'It meant a lot to get his approval. I feel valued.' - 'I felt like I mattered to him.'
Collaboration	- 'She could inspire me to get involved.' - 'It was about shared conversations.' - 'It's good when they ask for my ideas and advice.' - 'She took people on a journey with her.' - 'He could embrace and leverage the community resources.' - 'He was able to draw out the expertise of the team before making a decision.'

Attribute	Quote
Purpose	• 'Repeated key messages.' • 'Talks about the big picture.' • 'He had an eye on the horizon.' • 'He knew our purpose.' • 'She had a strong strategic direction.' • 'She talked about the vision a lot.'
Challenge	• 'He coached me.' • 'He challenged me.' • 'She held people to account.' • 'She was an excellent mentor.' • 'She asked thought-provoking questions and made me reflect and think for myself.' • 'He provided candid feedback.'
Communication	• 'She was a good listener.' • 'She had clear and honest communication.' • 'He was a master communicator.' • 'She didn't talk at us.' • 'I felt like he was there just for me. He always paid attention and took an interest when I talked to him, even though I know he had a lot on his mind.' • 'He could make meaning.'
Autonomy	• 'He did not micromanage me.' • 'It is motivating when someone has an expertise and are allowed to get on with their job.' • 'He gave me latitude to find my way in the project.' • 'Being afforded trust and autonomy forms you as a leader.' • 'After agreeing on some non-negotiables, he let me go and left me to do the job.'

Table 7: What schools said

Redefining leadership

There are thousands of definitions of leadership in the literature, but not one fully captured my findings and understanding of school leadership, so I looked to Feser (2016) and Ochsner and Lieberman (2001) to build on my research findings to shape a definition that captured school leadership, outlined as follows:

*A leader is someone who can inspire an uplifting **influence** on the intellect, emotion and energy through their behaviours, words, and tone to **grow other leaders** around them. It is a social influence, occurring through biological processes manifesting in the brain informed by a set of **attributes** that appeal to the inner **motivations**. They understand the need to inspire trust, build rapport and stimulate growth through adjusting their approach to align with how the **brain** operates to bring about positive **visionary change**. They make others shine. (Newman, 2022)*

If you are going to lead in the people business in a context of complexity and uncertainty, then it is essential to have clarity around what leadership is and looks like to you. As illustrated in the definition, there are a number of key terms that represent the essence of leadership, including influence, growing other leaders, attributes, motivation, understanding the brain and visionary change, hence the organisation of the content in this book. Just as we have a pedagogical framework for our schools to anchor into, decision-making for leadership can be much more coherent and aligned with a conceptual framework such as that shown in Figure 5 (overleaf).

The model is foregrounded with purpose, visions, values and beliefs as the starting point and shows the central focus of the 12 leadership attributes that can strengthen a leader's influence to inspire, unite and deliver. These building blocks will maximise contribute state and minimise agitate state, uplifting the team's intellect, emotion and energy, resulting in positive change.

The pillars of the leadership approach incorporate understanding influence enablers, change management, data-informed decision-making, shifting cultures and building systems, maintaining perspective and meaning-making, understanding human motivation, wellbeing and investing time wisely. The hallmarks incorporate the learning conversations that every leader can use to build capacity and other leaders around them, including managing conversations, mentoring conversations and coaching conversations.

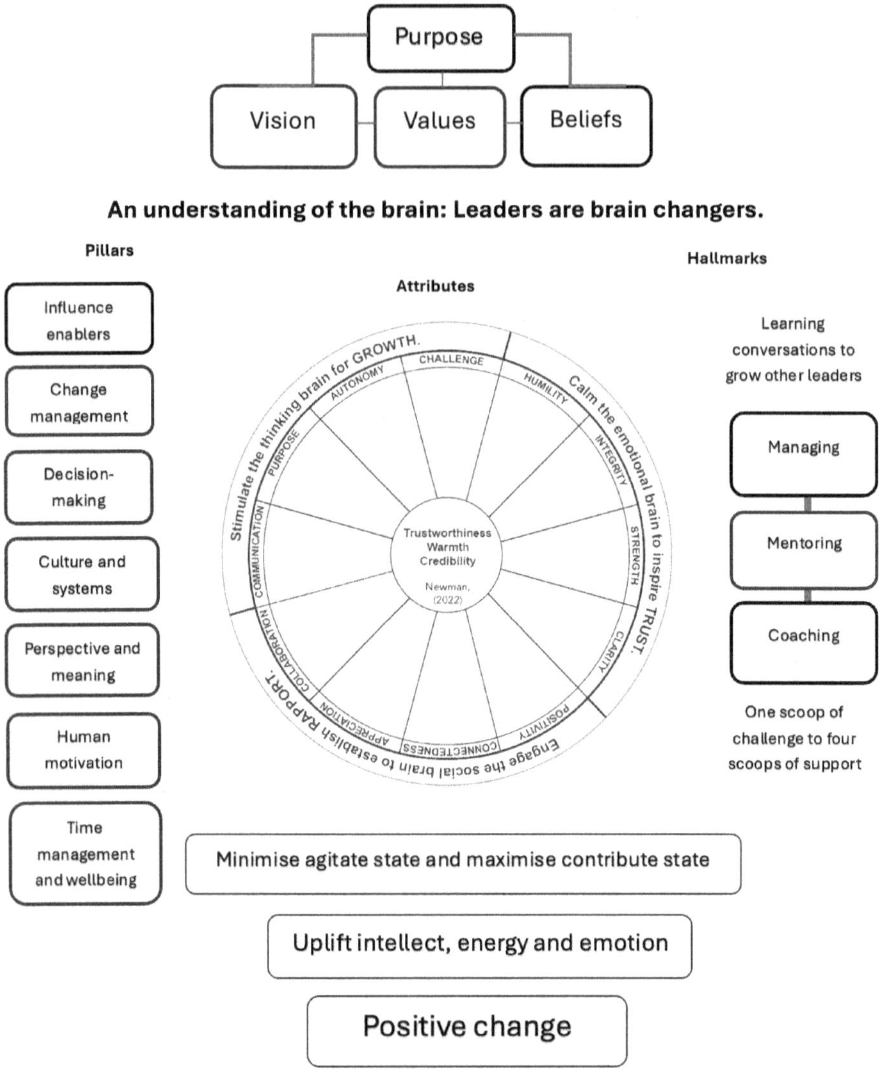

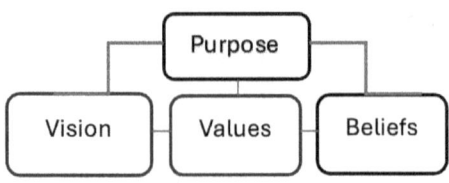

Figure 5: Leadership conceptual framework

Motivation and influence

In the article 'Why great leaders inspire instead of motivate', Levin (2017) states that a study by the *Harvard Business Review* surveyed over 5000 leaders and found that the ability to inspire stood out as one of the most important competencies of a leader today. It is a trait that creates the highest levels of engagement and is what separates the most effective leaders from others. It is what employers want most in their leaders (Horwitch & Chipple-Callahan, 2016).

One of the most dominant speakers on leadership inspiration in the literature is Sir Richard Branson. In his speech at the 63rd SHRM Annual Conference in Las Vegas (Gallo, 2011) he recommended hiring the type of leaders who 'inspire' their teams, and went on to say that inspiration is in 'short supply'. He quoted a range of studies, including a Gallup Poll (2011) which surveyed 2400 employees, showing that without inspiration, employees are demoralised, disinterested and disengaged.

A link between relational leaders and their ability to inspire for effective leadership has been shown in a study using scanning technology (Schaufenbuel, 2014). The study found that when staff interacted with a 'resonant relational leader' – someone they respected and were inspired by – 14 regions of the brain were activated. The active regions of the brain included areas associated with exciting attention (anterior cingulate cortex), social and emotional networks (right inferior frontal gyrus), mirror neurons (right inferior parietal lobe) and other regions associated with the approach response (right putamen; bilateral insula). When asked to recall events and conversations with leaders they were not inspired by, referred to as 'dissonant leaders', only six regions of the brain were activated and 11 regions were deactivated. Dissonant leaders deactivated the limbic systems in regard to the social systems (posterior cingulate cortex) and neural circuitry associated with mirror systems (left inferior frontal gyrus). The regions of the brain that were activated included regions associated with narrowing attention (bilateral anterior cingulate cortex), lowering compassion (left posterior cingulate cortex) and triggering negative emotion (posterior inferior frontal gyrus) (Boyatzis, 2012; Schaufenbuel, 2014).

Dopamine has a key role in motivation

Dopamine is a neurotransmitter that has a key role in motivation. The first time you do something or achieve something you get a dopamine hit, which reinforces associated networks, increasing the likelihood of repeating the behaviour. The next time you repeat it, dopamine is released as you head towards the goal, which is why it feels good but not nearly as good as the first time you did it. When you give up, a neuropeptide called nociceptin is released, and its receptors cancel or flush away any remaining dopamine, so you lose all motivation (Parker et al., 2019). To reset motivation levels, refocus on the why and the goal to restart the dopamine release (Parker et al., 2019).

Be mindful that you don't only get a dopamine hit when you are motivated to go for your walk, but you also get one when you sit down and stay on the couch. You put your shoes on and change into walking clothes, which turns on the dopamine drip. However, if you get interrupted or lose your focus, and sit down on the couch to eat a packet of chips, you will get another dopamine hit to keep you there. This dopamine takes a different neural path, and you don't want to reinforce that pathway. You have 30 seconds to act on your motivation, so act your way into motivation, don't wait. Dopamine has a role in motivating teams.

Motivating and neuroplasticity

Motivating teams to change means shifting thinking for new collective behaviours. This requires the brain to learn. Learning requires neurons to fire and strengthen neural pathways, encode new information, and consolidate it into memory. As stated previously, there will be limited changes in behaviour or learning without neuroplastic changes in the brain over time. Learning is about closing the gap between our current knowledge and an improved brain map. If we are always open to learning, then we are continually improving and updating our brain software. Words can influence thinking and feelings and by adjusting behaviours will help shift belief systems that lead to change.

The brain rewires daily in response to our experiences to prepare for the future it predicts. There are a number of ways the brain can change form over time. The neuroplastic changes in the brain are shown in Table 8.

Change	Description
Dendrite growth	The development of branches off the end of the neuron. The more dendrites, the more information that can be collected.
Spine growth	Nodules swell out of the dendrite branches where the neurotransmitter docks into the receptors.
Myelination	The coating around the shaft of the axon is called myelin. The thicker the myelin, the faster the thinking.

Change	Description
Neurogenesis	The development of new neurons.
Density, strengthening and connectivity	The synaptic connections peak by six to eight years. As we age, the brain density thins, refines and eventually becomes more rigid. As repetition strengthens the synaptic connections, they become more efficient, providing multiple pathways to collect information.
Sensitivity and precision	Strengthening the sensitivity and precision of receptors makes collecting the information more efficient (Gluck et al., 2016; Gordon, 2022).
Epigenetics	This is about genetic control factors other than the DNA sequence. Chemical compounds and environmental factors can change genetic function across generations (Cluck et al., 2016).
Ephatic transmission	This is an electromagnetic synaptic transmission rather than a chemical and electrical one. It is 5000 times faster than neural firing (*Scientific American*, 8 November 2024).
Pruning	During sleep unused dendrites are pruned. In this way the brain adapts and refines.

Table 8: The brain rewires

This ability of the brain to change shape and form in response to the environment is called *neuroplasticity*. There are numerous studies that show evidence of neuroplasticity today, but the concept has its origins in a theory developed by Gerald Edelman (1978) called Neural Darwinism. Everything we think, do, or feel through experience changes the brain as it strengthens and shapes neural pathways to prepare for future experiences (Gordon, 2022). For example, as the principal and staff members interact in a conversation, each of their brains will be responding to the nature of that interaction and changing, establishing mental maps to form their world view. The mental maps shape and make meaning of the information coming in. As the same thoughts and feelings are continually experienced, our beliefs and values become increasingly dominant and hardwired. Once the neural circuitry is networked, the brain will search for existing wiring, so new thought processes will link to existing neural circuitry, reinforcing what we think we know, which in turn drives our actions. This is why individuals make assumptions as they receive information, as the new data or learning links to prior learning to save brain fuel. Making assumptions with only some of the information which distorts our thinking is called cognitive bias. As our belief systems are also neuron pathways, this makes changing our thinking challenging and purposeful work. The neuroplastic nature of the brain means that a leader can in some way impact the reshaping of beliefs and thinking and therefore change collective behaviours.

In his book *Immersion* (2022), Paul Zak shares his research into what happens in a 'memorable moment', taking blood tests and brain scans. He found that it takes:

- Attention
- An emotional response
- Drop of dopamine
- Release of oxytocin.

A leader can create the conditions to maximise memorable moments with this in mind. Everything they say will have an effect on the brain of the listener and, more importantly, on motivation levels, as the impact of a conversation leaves the listener with a feeling (such as, inspiration, anger, disappointment or joy). Changing thinking involves learning for behaviour change.

Takeaways

- Our innate traits are either amplified or minimised as we learn and experience events.
- We all have different starting points on the leadership journey.
- A leader needs to be highly self-aware to know their impact on others.
- Emotion is at the heart of social interaction.
- We need to be fully present to problem-solve or learn, rather than be on autopilot.

- The way we feel about someone will either inhibit or enable our willingness to engage at our best.
- A leader needs to be able to change brain states at critical times.
- The emotional brain is hardwired to detect threat.
- The social brain evolved to operate in and belong to a group.
- The thinking brain has an innate desire to learn and achieve.
- We are attracted to like-minded people. This is more about their standard of conduct than their cultural background.
- The emotional brain has been called the honest brain, and the thinking brain has been called the lying brain.
- The three brains are interrelated and sequential, meaning a leader needs to calm the brain stem to build trust and rapport in order to stimulate growth.
- To make rational decisions, the brain needs to be calm and composed.
- Trust and communication have a tendency to decline as the group increases in size.
- Understand that brain state is connected to wellness.
- Learn how to change channels on your own remote control to channel up or down.
- There are 12 leadership attributes that inspire and motivate others for best performance.
- There is limited behaviour change without neuroplastic changes in the brain over time.
- Our attention is hooked by anything funny, unusual, unexpected, novel, important, interesting or pleasurable.
- The workplace culture will either speed up or slow down what you want to achieve.
- When we are spent, we are on cognitive, emotional and sensory overload.
- Leadership influence is embodied in a positive connection that reveals emotion which inspires an insight into changed thinking.

Reflection and journaling

- What ideas emerged?
- What are your insights and learnings?
- What are your challenges?
- What was confirming?
- What is now clearer for you?
- What will you now do differently?
- What is the one most important thing you will do next?

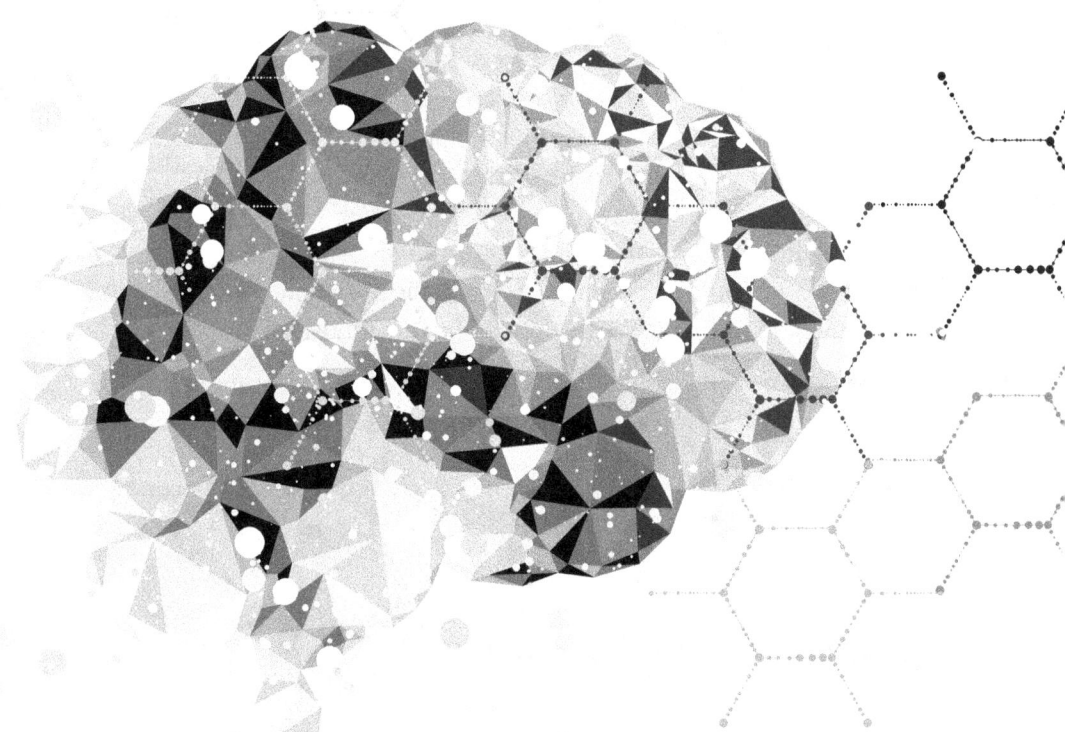

Part 2
The 12 Leadership Attributes

'People need leadership.
Everything else can be managed.'

ANON.

Who we are is how we lead

As outlined above, my recent research (Newman, 2022) identified 12 leadership attributes that can either inspire and unite or demotivate a team. The attributes shown in Figure 6 define the behaviours of an influential leader. Influence is earned, not given with the principal's badge. It is inherent in who we are and how we turn up. The meaning is shown in the words within each category. Table 9 is a reflective tool which outlines questions for each of the leadership attributes.

There are three major categories: 'Calm the emotional brain to inspire TRUST', 'Engage the social brain to establish RAPPORT' and 'Stimulate the thinking brain for GROWTH'.

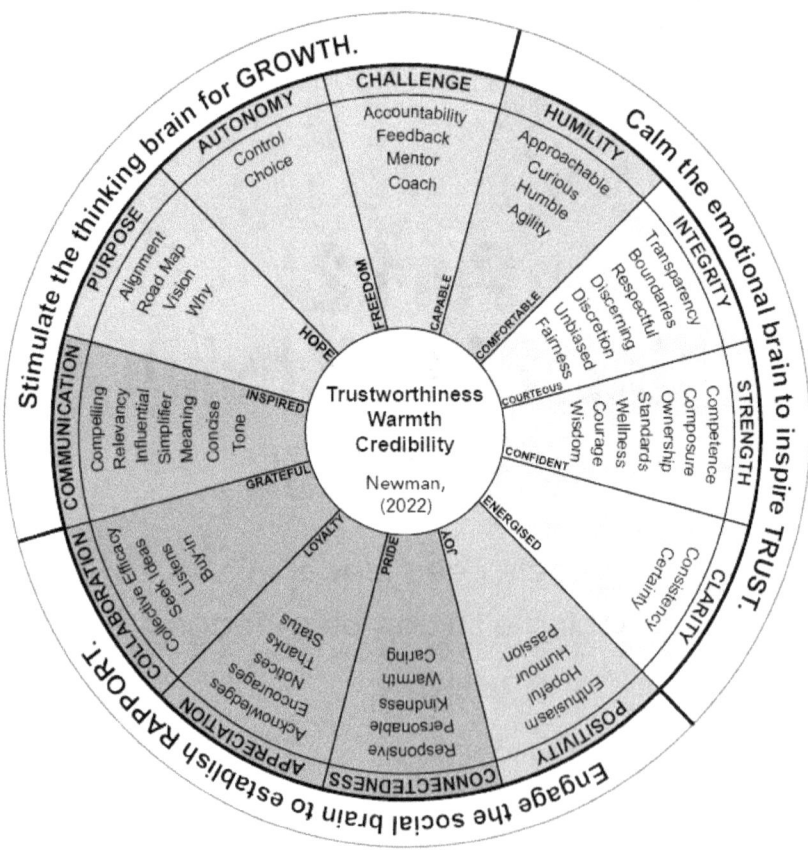

Figure 6: The 12 Leadership Attributes (Newman, 2022)

About	What is your confidence level with your ability to...
Humility	
Approachability Curiosity Agility Humility Teachability Adaptability	• Inspire trust by being approachable? • Be self-reflective and often seek feedback from others? • Be highly curious and ask more questions than make statements? • Be coachable? • Adapt and pivot to changing circumstances in complex times?
Integrity	
Transparency Boundaries Respect Trust Discerning Discretion Unbiased Fairness Protective	• Be fair, honest and respectful? • Live by cast-iron values? • Know when to draw a line in the sand and speak up? • Discern what is right? • Know and action your values and virtues? • Care about humans and their wellbeing? • Be a truth seeker? • Inspire trust in others? • Make values-driven decisions?
Strength	
Competence Composure Ownership Standards Wellness Discipline Courage Wisdom	• Put courage over comfort? • Be up to date with the research and highly competent? • Confront active blockers? • Be calm and composed under pressure? • Call behaviour? • Own your own behaviour? • Be self-disciplined around your own wellbeing? • Show valour? • Recover from setbacks, stay on course with resistance and overcome obstacles? • Build interpersonal courage?
Clarity	
Consistency Certainty Perspective	• Clarify roles, articulate results and expectations? • Tame the bureaucracy? • Embed consistent practices? • Share a decision-making model to show who, how and why decisions are made? • Implement strategic systems for meetings and problem-solving? • Cut through the noise for perspective?

About	What is your confidence level with your ability to...
Positivity	
Enthusiasm Hopefulness Humour Passion Potential Beauty	• Use the language of hope and set the tone? • Celebrate success together? • Show enthusiasm and passion for the work? • Demonstrate a growth mindset? • Catch people doing the right thing? • See potential and the beauty in things? • Drive continuous improvement?
Connectedness	
Responsive Personability Warmth Caring Empathy	• Show warmth and build relationships? • Be responsive to other people's needs? • Build a unique proud tribe?
Appreciation	
Acknowledgment Encouragement Noticing Thanking Status Kindness	• Care about, encourage and protect others up and down the line? • Notice others to build their status? • Say 'thank you' often? • Be generous? • Avoid pre-judgments and show kindness?
Collaboration	
Efficacy Seek ideas Listen Extract expertise Ownership Unite Inclusivity Motivate	• See other perspectives and listen to all the voices? • Build collective ownership and collective efficacy? • Draw on the collective expertise of the group? • Focus on the collective success? • Unite rather than divide? • Leverage cultural and community resources?
Communication	
Compelling Relevance Influence Simplify Conciseness	• Make the complex message simple and compelling? • Have candid conversations? • Inspire thinking for changed behaviour? • Be decisive when appropriate? • Use 'pass the salt' tone consistently?

About	What is your confidence level with your ability to...
Tone Storytelling Connecting Proactive and responsive Meaning-making	• Use strategic phrases for impact? • Be an agent of change through learning conversations? • Listen to learn and connect rather than listen to defend or boost? • Tell engaging stories for teachable moments? • Prime conversational chemistry? • Ask questions to build leadership thinking in others? • Clearly communicate strategic planning and make meaning clear?
Purpose	
Alignment Road map Vision Why Strategic Deliver	• Articulate a clear vision of a preferred future? • Align roles with purpose? • Keep the team focus on the priorities and the right work? • Explain the why often? • Create symbolism? • See the whole and the moving parts and their connections? • Strategise to influence outcomes and shape desired behaviours?
Challenge	
Accountability Feedback Mentorship Coaching Learning	• Coach and grow others? • Keep others accountable for their own results? • Provide opportunities for training? • Use 'show me not tell me'? • Share self-talk at teachable moments? • Differentiate your leadership style to manage, mentor and coach? • Continue your learning? • Notice and develop the potential of others?
Autonomy	
Control Choice	• Share your leadership? • Allow people the space to do their jobs within the rules of engagement? • Do only what you should be doing?

Table 9: The leadership attribute reflective tool

The leadership attribute reflective tool

Reflect on the above table and assess your confidence levels with each leadership attribute. Ask yourself, on a scale of 1–10 (1–3 you are still learning and 8–10 you have mastered the skill set), how would you rate yourself? What are your strengths? Identify your gaps. Have you any areas of development? What can you do differently to build more powerful habits?

1–3   Learning
4–5   Developing
6–7   Confident
8–9   Habitual
10   Mastered

The 12 leadership attributes can be perceived as a threat response or a reward response. Table 10 outlines the behaviours that bring about an agitated state or a contribution state. A leader who understands that these behaviours have a neuroscientific basis can adjust their behaviours to align with how the brain operates to maximise cooperation and engagement levels.

The next chapters will unpack each attribute, share stories of leadership in action, outline the findings of relevant studies, and provide tools incorporating practical strategies you can use the next day.

> 'To be persuasive, we must be believable.
> To be believable, we must be credible.
> To be credible, we must be truthful.'
> Edward R. Murrow

Agitate state	Attribute	Contribute state
Egocentric, confrontational, know-it-all. Needs to be right or win all the time.	Humility	Approachable, curious, humble, able to be vulnerable, real, seeks feedback, tries to improve daily, is highly self-aware, grasps agility.

Agitate state	Attribute	Contribute state
Insincerity, gossiping, biased, unfair, blames others for their errors.	Integrity	Fair, respectful, role model, discreet, honest, discerning.
People pleaser, incompetent, weak, swayed by peer pressure, avoids difficult issues. Lack of self-discipline to maintain wellness. Caves under peer pressure.	Strength	Visible, persuasive, tough-minded, competent, calm under pressure, courage over comfort. Addresses difficult issues, owns behaviour. Role model of fitness/wellness.
Inconsistent messages and behaviours, confusing.	Clarity	Clear expectations of role and results required. Consistent behaviours and clear decision-making model. Has clarity of purpose.
Negative with fixed mindset, takes themselves too seriously, only comments on the things that go wrong.	Positivity	Hopeful language, uses sense of humour, shows passion for the work, positive, enthusiastic, growth mindset, celebrates the things that go right.
Cold, aloof, puts product before people, is task-orientated.	Connectedness	Shows warmth, personable, builds rapport and invests time in getting to know the human behind the role, shows compassion and is responsive to people's emotional needs.
Corrects in public, never says thank you or writes thank you notes. Only ever provides critical feedback based on their own projected fears.	Appreciation	Notices and comments on people's strengths and achievements, says thank you, praises in public, builds the status of others. Provides four times more acknowledgment and encouragement than critique.
Never seeks team's ideas and perspectives. What they say has very little impact on changed thinking and behaviour.	Collaboration	Seeks team's ideas and perspective before big decisions are made. Can build collective buy-in. Creates a setting to maximise collaboration.

Agitate state	Attribute	Contribute state
Avoids candid conversations. Waffly and boring speeches. Spreads confusion and defensiveness.	Communication	Is a compelling and master communicator who gets people's attention, is an active listener, can simplify complex messages, seeks and gives feedback. Clear, concise, relevant and true. Uses a toolkit of strategic phrases to diffuse tension and maximise impact.
Forgets to reinforce the why. Doesn't keep the team on track with the important work. Is distracted with shiny new things.	Purpose	Can explain a clear vision and everyone understands how their role aligns with the bigger picture. Has a road map to get there. Focused on the right work.
Never reads a book, does not hold others accountable for their role, always tells, never asks, does not provide training.	Challenge	Coaches team members to build other leaders. Provides feedback, provides opportunity for growth for team members, lifelong learner.
Micromanaging at the risk of squashing innovation.	Autonomy	Allows others some sense of autonomy in their role, matches people with their passions and fit.

Table 10: Threat and reward behaviours

Reflection and journaling

- What ideas emerged?
- What are your insights and learnings?
- What are your challenges?
- What was confirming?
- What is now clearer for you?
- What will you now do differently?
- What is the one most important thing you will do next?

LEADERSHIP ATTRIBUTE 1: HUMILITY

> *'If you think leadership is about you,
> you will be a temporary leader.'*
> Major General Steven Day

Stay curious and approachable

Humility is about being modest, not showy or pretentious. Authenticity beats perfection. It is an overarching category that captures approachability, accessibility, willingness to be vulnerable, curiosity and being open to learning. Humility rises to the top when it comes to leadership attributes that inspire. In his book *Good to Great* (2001) Jim Collins found that high-performance CEOs showed two qualities: 'professional will', a passion for the work, and humility. The *Washington Post* (2016) reports that 56 per cent of 5th and 6th graders believe that 'the humble are embarrassed, sad, lonely and shy'. This suggests that they think showing humility is weak. This is far from the truth. It takes significant courage and strength to be humble as a leader. However, they also report that leaders are more powerful when they are humble, having lower staff turnover and higher employee satisfaction.

At the heart of humility is a willingness to be curious, questioning to learn, and challenging long-held assumptions. Curious leaders have the ability to reshape their thinking as new information comes in. A study by Gino (2018) examined 3000 employees and found that 92 per cent of them valued curiosity in the workplace. They associated curiosity with higher motivation, good performance and job satisfaction. However, 70 per cent of the workforce experienced barriers to asking questions in the workplace. As I visit schools and businesses, people will sometimes confide that they once gave freely of their ideas, asking for help and feedback, but now hold back because of the negative response they received from one of the leaders. This would indicate that organisations need to build psychologically safe settings where individuals can speak up without feeling judged or shut down.

It seems that children as young as five develop intuitions about how they are perceived. Good and Shaw's (2022) research showed that five-year-olds avoid asking for help in school for fear of being embarrassed. By the age of seven, children begin seeing a correlation between not seeking help and looking competent in front of others. Harvard Professor Amy Edmondson, author of *The Fearless Organisation* (2019), explains we may fear asking questions because we don't want to question our boss's judgment, look stupid, be perceived as negative, or be viewed as incompetent or the squeaky wheel. In my research, teachers reported that they wanted to ask a question at a meeting but they held back because they thought everyone would think they should know the answer.

Leaders are teachable

Humility is about being open to learning and being curious. According to Marty Samples (2024), only 42 per cent of professionals believe they are highly teachable and 98 per cent of chief executive officers stated that they look for teachability in their employees and feel it is important. Marty says, 'Teachability isn't about intelligence. It's about adaptability, humility and a hunger to grow. It's about being open to learn, unlearn and relearn.' There are ways you can show you are teachable, including:

- Seek feedback not only on the technical matters but also on your interpersonal skills.
- Listen more and ask questions rather than tell.
- Be curious and open to learning.
- Reflect on your impact on others.
- Consider all sides of the story.
- Consider errors as a learning opportunity.
- Stay humble; you are showing you don't know everything.
- Identify where your starting point is and where you want to go.
- Give the talker your full attention.
- Say, 'What makes you say that?'

Allow others to shine

The most frequent aspect of humility raised by teachers in interviews was that they were inspired by principals who were approachable and were not afraid to show their vulnerability, especially when there was disagreement. Leaders don't always understand the weight of their position, and team members may not feel comfortable questioning their leader (Willink & Babin, 2017, p. 81). An influential leader is not intimidated when they are outshone by a team member or when a team member knows more about something than they do. They know that it is important to draw out the collective expertise of the team for sound decision-making and growth. It is essential to be flexible and adaptable as new information comes in and be prepared to change one's views as new ideas from the team are considered and counter evidence is presented (Robinson et al., 2008). Humility is also about being able to say sorry when an error is made and resisting the desire to be right and win all the time. It could be inferred from studies that people are repelled by a leader who plays oneupmanship and attracted to a leader who is humbler.

Evan Daniel, a retired school principal, exemplifies the concept of humility. He views leadership as a privilege, not an entitlement. In our conversations it is clear that he does not think of himself as different, above or better than those he was leading. He stated, 'I viewed everyone in the school community as having an important and equal role, including parents, cleaners, groundsmen, myself, office workers and teachers'. He said he participated in working bees, fun races, school camps and fancy dress balls, picked up litter and unblocked toilets. 'I tried to set an example. Towards the end of my career, I began to think of myself as the most highly paid teacher in the school. It was my role to support teachers so that they could teach without interruptions and were well resourced. If someone made an error, I felt it was my job to back them, discussing the situation after we resolved things together.' Evan moved around the state to a number of schools that benefited from his expertise. His former school communities talk about him with respect and fondness.

Lessons from the front line

I was privileged to meet Major General Stephen Day at a police forum where we were the keynote speakers. Major General Day is a highly decorated two star general who has been a government adviser on leadership and cybersecurity after four decades in the military and on active duty. Day (2015) emphasises in his leadership speeches that humility is an important attribute for leaders. In his article 'Lessons from the front line' he provides examples from his deep lived experience while leading under fire. I was struck by his humble manner and keen curiosity. He exudes a calm strength that made me feel safe. When he discussed the topic of leadership, he didn't talk about the mechanics of operation but rather the fundamental human challenges and personal attributes of leadership. He discussed the time he led a team into the Australian bush and got lost, stating that all he had to do was take his ego out and ask his team where they were, but he didn't, and as a result he said that he and the whole team spent another unnecessary uncomfortable night in the bush without comforts. Major General Day went on to explain that humility is a core character trait of leadership and that it must come from the leader first, to inspire others to do the same. It is not easy to show what feels like weakness when others look up to you for strength. I know that his words have had a positive influence on many other leaders, inspiring reflection on their own behaviours.

Agility takes adaptability and flexibility

If you looked up a definition of agility, you might find that it refers to the ability to move, think and understand quickly. Its connection with humility gives it a slightly different meaning. When things get tricky, and they are not going your way, it may be easy to get frustrated or even angry with the person or task you are dealing with. However, this reaction isn't going to get you far in leadership and it usually doesn't solve the problem, because that would be black-and-white thinking. Things are never that simple. In my role as a consultant, I interface with different states, systems and roles. They all have their own expectations and hidden rules.

I have learnt that my expectations can sometimes get in the way. For example, when I work in a school, I understand the hidden rules and roles of staff. I always find that the principal is proactive around my needs and vice versa, because we understand each other. If there is any tension, I can usually avoid stepping on toes, because I intuitively know what to expect. However, when I am working with another agency, and go with the same expectations about what should or should not happen, I might be disappointed, but it won't be their fault. It falls back onto me to reflect on the role of that person and whether they had the authority to say yes in the first place. Leadership is about being able to adapt and flex with a resilient response. Sometimes expectations, agendas, rules and roles differ and therefore you need to tailor and be fluid in your response so you don't allow the response to become part of the problem. This takes a considerable amount of humility.

Understand your limitations

Part of humility is being in touch with your own skill set and shortcomings. Research by Ultimate Software (2017) highlighted that leaders don't always have a grasp on what their teams think of them. They found leaders often overestimated their leadership skill due to over-confidence and under-training:

- 71 per cent of leaders stated that they knew how to motivate their teams, but only 44 per cent of team members reported that their leaders knew how to motivate them.
- 80 per cent of leaders said they were transparent in how they dealt with their line managers, but only 55 per cent of team members agreed with that.
- 75 per cent of leaders said they were approachable, but only 50 per cent of team members reported that they had an approachable manager.

The Dunning-Kruger effect might shed some light on why this is so. This is when a lack of skill or knowledge causes people to over-estimate their competence because they don't know enough yet to detect where they lie on the capability curve. Another interesting matter associated with accidental arrogance is when a little bit of knowledge can be dangerous. I was told recently that a school had banned handwritten note-taking because someone had read that handwriting was associated with multi-tasking and it was a poor learning habit. As a result, the school banned all handwriting and mandated keyboard-only use. This is an example of too little information getting in the way.

The higher your leadership position, the less it is about you and the more it is about serving others and creating a setting where others can lead. The more power you are perceived as having, the less likely it is that others will tell you the truth. The more experienced you become, the higher the risk of developing blind spots. Unless you have a high level of self-awareness around your strengths and weaknesses, your team will:

- Use self-protective behaviours around you.
- Warn new team members about your triggers.
- Approach you in impression-management mode.
- Build processes to work around you.
- Discuss your flaws, because that is all they will see.
- Rehearse before they tell you bad news.
- Avoid telling you what you need to hear, even though everyone else knows.

Consider the feedback that hurts and find the pattern that reveals the truth hidden in the perception. Ask:

- What am I missing here?
- What am I doing to amplify or block my influence?
- What needs to be said that has been unsaid?
- What is my story?
- What is it like to spend 5 minutes with me?

Humility-based leadership

Dr Evian Gordon, founder of the first and largest international human brain database, Total Brain, is someone I admire. His humility, shown in his prevailing sentiment of warmth (heart leadership), curiosity (head leadership) and intuitive foresight (gut leadership), and his willingness to share his expertise and guidance, have been pivotal for me in my leadership growth. To me, Evian is the father of integrated neuroscience. When I reached out to him as a PhD candidate, a stranger to him at the time, he took the time to ring me from California to encourage my work. It is not surprising that when I asked Evian what comes to mind when he thinks of leadership influence he chose not to think of himself but of a story illustrating a colleague's humility.

He talks about Peter Cooper with great respect. Peter is the founder of Cooper Investors, the most successful value-latency investment company in Australia. Evian says:

When someone has a 30-year track record of success and over $10 billion of investments, it would not be surprising to me if they tended towards arrogance. In Peter's case, I was fascinated by the depth and breadth of his growth mindset. This was coupled with his interest in understanding how the brain's unconscious and conscious brain pattern recognition decision-making and biases played out. Also, how to reconcile AI predictive analytics and human brain expert pattern recognition. He embraced styles of thinking from different personality types but also with respect to different cultural influences of Western rationality and Eastern interconnected perspectives. He has a profound humility in embracing this complexity and his relentless determination to create a humility-centric culture in his organisation. The authentic depth of that humility lesson from Peter Cooper inspires me in all that I try to achieve.

Takeaways

- Influential leaders resist the urge to be right and win all the time.
- Showing vulnerability takes courage.
- Does my behaviour project my intent and strengths or my fears and ego?
- Being open to learning, unlearning and relearning is important.
- Leadership can be paradoxical, and leaders need to be able to navigate the grey.
- Leaders seek feedback; they don't wait for it to come to them.
- Leadership is about serving others rather than yourself.
- Influential leaders can take their ego out.
- Don't allow your response to become part of the problem.
- Be curious first; don't jump in to judge.
- Leaders understand their limitations.

Reflection and journaling

- What ideas emerged?
- What are your insights and learnings?
- What are your challenges?
- What was confirming?
- What is now clearer for you?
- What will you now do differently?
- What is the one most important thing you will do next?

LEADERSHIP ATTRIBUTE 2: INTEGRITY

> *'People need to believe in the person before they believe in their ideas.'*
> John Maxwell

Set the standard and the tone

Integrity is an overarching word that captures honesty, fairness, strong boundaries, inclusivity, values-driven, sincerity, discretion, role-modelling, keeping confidences, being unbiased and openness. It is not surprising that teachers reported this attribute as the most important, as a strong sense of integrity builds credibility and inspires trust. A team can detect subtle cues in the leader's tone, interpersonals, words and actions that may or may not match meaning and agendas. Any misalignment can erode trust, and that distrust will be reflected back, sending off a misalignment signal in the brain. The dopaminergic systems are activated when the brain perceives that we have been treated fairly; the same brain areas are activated when we drink wine or eat ice-cream. Teams look to the leader for clues on how to behave and notice when the leader is willing to take the more difficult path of what is right, fair, good and true despite the alternatives that may be more popular, quicker or easier.

Leaders with high integrity tend to have more peace of mind, because if you tell the truth you have nothing to hide. Telling the truth when it is tough builds resilience. If our words match our behaviours, we have anchored our decisions into cast-iron values. Showing consistent values in behaviour is role-modelling what you want to see in others.

*'Example is not the main thing in influencing others,
it is the only thing.'*
Albert Schweitzer

The dropped lolly

Young people often have a clear sense of integrity, even if it starts as a simple understanding of right and wrong. I remember being about ten years old, standing at the counter of a lolly shop across from my primary school, a place that's long since gone. I had chosen Red Moons, my favourite. Back then, the shopkeeper would count each lolly, taken from a large glass jar using metal tongs, dropping them one by one into a small white paper bag. As she reached six, one slipped and rolled onto the dusty counter. I watched as the sticky red lolly picked up a layer of grime. She picked it up, ready to drop it into my packet. I spoke up: 'You can have that one.' With a grimace, she replied, 'Oh no, thank you, it's been on the counter.' I smiled, looked her in the eye, and said, 'You were going to ask me to eat it.'

At the time, I felt bold, maybe even a tad cheeky, but in hindsight, I see it differently. That was a moment when I was finding my voice, learning to stand up for what felt right. In leadership, there's no room for 'lolly moments'. When we're in positions of influence, watched, judged and followed, our values must align with our actions. A true leader knows their values intimately, and those values show not only in their behaviour but also in what they choose to tolerate.

The wounded leader

Integrity is tested when we are leading in a dysfunctional system or with a dysfunctional boss. Tom Browning is a commercial pilot with a military background and, when asked about what leadership means to him, he tells a story that talks of positioning the team first. He believes this is especially important in the face of a toxic workplace culture where not all leaders at all levels align with the same leadership philosophy. He states that leadership is simple but its consistent execution is extremely difficult. Tom believes it is based predominantly on two values: integrity and tenacity. He explains that integrity refers to the unyielding pursuit of whatever is in the best moral and ethical interest of the team and its operational functions. Tenacity refers to the upholding of integrity in the execution of the mission during the broad range of sustained assaults made upon it by forces of corporate avarice or relentless self-promotion by senior organisational personnel.

Tom explains that leadership begins with the genuine belief that the collective wellbeing of the team is more important than any particular individual interests within it and significantly more important than the leader. It is only through selfless devotion to this concept that true leadership can exist. It must be genuine. Some can fake it for a while but they will not stand the 'heat of battle' very long. Worthy team members who share a collective vision can sense a disingenuous leader almost instantly.

Tom says that in pursuit of the team's wellbeing and progression the leader will sometimes be placed in situations where the organisational pressures are deemed an unacceptable burden on their team. Demonstrating the required integrity and tenacity to navigate these confrontations and defend the group will have mixed results. When the battle is won, the team may never know the true cost to the leader in terms of effort and pain. Nonetheless, the tenacious leader may be wounded (figuratively) but would never have compromised their integrity or that of their team. With this strength of character, it is no surprise that Tom's team would follow him anywhere. Tom's story reminds us that just because you are in a dysfunctional team does not mean you are dysfunctional. Additionally, if you have a dysfunctional boss, you are likely to get wounded and it might be time to leave.

Live your values

This is an exercise that can help clarify values and assess the alignment of values to behaviour. Some values are listed in Table 11.

1. List the ten most important things to you besides your family.
2. Identify your top three.
3. Now imagine you have won $2 million in the lottery – what would you do?
4. Now imagine you have a million dollars coming in each month and you have done everything in your wildest dreams. What would you be doing? Do you think that is what you should be doing?

Acceptance	Discovery	Integrity	Prosperity
Accountability	Discretion	Intelligence	Prudence
Achievement	Diversity	Intimacy	Punctuality
Adaptability	Drive	Joy	Realism
Advancement	Duty	Justice	Recognition
Adventure	Economy	Kindness	Relaxation
Altruism	Elegance	Knowledge	Reliability
Ambition	Empathy	Leadership	Religiousness
Appreciation	Encouragement	Learning	Reputation
Approval	Enjoyment	Liberty	Resilience
Assertiveness	Enthusiasm	Logic	Resourcefulness
Balance	Ethics	Love	Respect
Beauty	Excellence	Loyalty	Responsibility
Belonging	Excitement	Mastery	Rigour
Boldness	Exploration	Modesty	Security
Brilliance	Fairness	Motivation	Selflessness
Calmness	Faith	Nature	Sensitivity
Candour	Fame	Neatness	Sensuality
Care	Fitness	Nonconformity	Service
Certainty	Focus	Obedience	Sharing
Charity	Frankness	Openness	Simplicity
Cheerfulness	Freedom	Optimism	Sincerity
Clarity	Friendship	Orderliness	Solidarity
Cleanliness	Fun	Organisation	Sophistication
Comfort	Gallantry	Originality	Stability
Compassion	Generosity	Passion	Stillness
Competence	Grace	Patience	Strength
Competition	Growth	Peace	Teamwork
Conformity	Happiness	Perfection	Thoughtfulness
Connection	Harmony	Perkiness	Tranquillity
Contribution	Health	Perseverance	Trust
Control	Holiness	Persistence	Truth
Courage	Honesty	Philanthropy	Unflappability
Courtesy	Hopefulness	Playfulness	Uniqueness
Creativity	Humility	Poise	Valour
Credibility	Humour	Polish	Variety
Curiosity	Imagination	Popularity	Vision
Dependability	Independence	Power	Warmth
Determination	Individuality	Practicality	Wealth
Dignity	Influence	Pride	Wisdom
Diligence	Insightfulness	Privacy	Wonder
Discipline	Inspiration	Professionalism	

Table 11: Values

Trust and honesty

Kouzes and Posner (1990) found that honesty was reported in their surveys of over 7500 managers from a range of industries and organisations as the leading leadership characteristic, concluding that this is central to our need to trust a leader before we follow them onto the battlefield or into the boardroom or principal's office. Specifically, they reported that for a leader to be perceived as honest they had to be seen as truthful, ethical and principled. When they asked the teams how they measured trust, they said it was evident in the leader's behaviour.

The survey participants reported repeatedly that when the leader did what they said they were going to do and were consistent about living their own values, participants perceived them as honest and were more inclined to trust them. Cover-ups, taking credit for others' achievements, not following through, lying, breaking promises and inconsistency between word and action were all indications of a lack of honesty (Fehr et al., 1992; Newman, 2022). A dishonest leader is likely to violate a team's trust in their integrity, leading to the team's distrust of the leader (Garrett et al., 2016; Krasikova et al., 2013; Xu & Cooper Thomas, 2011).

Building trust

Trust is at the heart of integrity. There are hundreds of studies showing that trust is important in leader–follower relationships, but what does that look like for behaviour? The brain is hardwired to detect threat, so distrust is the default of the more primitive areas of the brain. A leader can't expect to be given trust by the team overnight, as trust needs to be earned. Additionally, leaders need to be worthy of that trust. Table 12 shows what trust behaviour looks like.

No.	Trust behaviour
1	Call behaviour. Address inappropriate or unhelpful behaviour.
2	Candid talk. Honest conversations don't mean you don't filter what you say. Say what is on your mind in a respectful way. However, be mindful that tact is sometimes not enough; you might have to be direct.
3	Clean intent. Check your agenda. Is it clean?
4	Confront reality. Address the elephants in the room.

No.	Trust behaviour
5	Competence. Master your expertise around your core business.
6	Compassion. Show enthusiasm for the work and empathy for the team.
7	Confidentiality. Keep confidences. Be discreet.
8	Connect respectfully. Be considerate of others.
9	Clarify expectations. How do people know how to behave if you don't highlight what you expect to see?
10	Courage to extend trust: The easiest way to build trust is to give trust.
11	Continue to listen. Don't make assumptions. Enquire and be present.
12	Commit to loyalty. Protect the team up and down the line of command. Support individuals when things go wrong. You have their back.
13	Correct errors. Learn from your mistakes. Say sorry when appropriate.
14	Commitment savvy. Do what you say you are going to do. Turning up is a big part of leadership support.
15	Confidence to share. Allow people to get to know you. Be open as much as your psychological comfort will allow.
16	Cooperation. Be a supportive team player.
17	Communication matches trust level. Tailor your conversation between too personal and too clinical.
18	Consistency. Humans love certainty as it makes them feel safe. If changing the goal posts, explain why. What you say needs to match what you do.

Table 12: Trust behaviours (Newman, 2020)

Communication matches trust level

Professor Dan McAdames explains that if we ask questions that are aimed at three levels of intimacy, we can break down the barriers we erect in working relationships. Conversations that remain at Level 1 will not deepen relationships or build trust. However, people need to feel psychologically safe to have Level 3 conversations that will galvanise and build loyalty and trust. These questions are shown in Table 13.

Level	Question type	Example
1	Around traits	Would you describe yourself as an extrovert?
2	Around goals, roles, skills and values	What are you passionate about? What is important to you in this role?
3	At the heart of our identity	What happened in your childhood that has made you who you are? What conversation do you need to have with yourself that you have been avoiding?

Table 13: Levels of questioning

Takeaways

- A leader's words align with their behaviour.
- Trust is expressed in the behaviours you see.
- Leaders have cast-iron values and anchor their decisions into them.
- Leaders take the more difficult path of what is right, fair, good and true, despite the alternative options that may be more popular, quicker or easier.
- Just because you are in a dysfunctional team, does not mean you are dysfunctional.
- Upholding your integrity within a dysfunctional system can involve leadership wounds.
- Values are shown not only in behaviour but in what you choose to tolerate.

Reflection and journaling

- What ideas emerged?
- What are your insights and learnings?
- What are your challenges?
- What was confirming?
- What is now clearer for you?
- What will you now do differently?
- What is the one most important thing you will do next?

LEADERSHIP ATTRIBUTE 3: STRENGTH

'As a leader you get what you tolerate.'
Susan Scott

Own your own space

Strength in the context of leadership is chiefly about character strength and is an overarching category for tough-mindedness, visibility, persuasive influence, upholding standards, wisdom, competency, self-discipline, and being calm and composed under pressure. Strong leaders understand that conflict is part of managing people. It is not about using a big stick and using positional power. As one principal in my study said, 'If you have to force your positional power to get things done, perhaps you don't have any power!' It is about personal power.

A leader owns their own space. Being clear about your values, purpose and role will make this easier when things get messy or you meet resistance, as it allows you to anchor into a place of certainty to make decisions. A strong leader in a big school can't avoid complaints along the way over the long term. It takes a certain level of confidence to make decisions and take action, when not everyone agrees. Confidence comes with competence. In fact, competence was the most reported component of strength desired by teachers, who stated that they wanted a principal with a firm grasp on the expertise associated with their role.

When Russia launched an invasion of Ukraine on 24 February 2022, the Ukrainian President Volodymyr Zelenskyy was reportedly offered evacuation by the United States. In response, he made his now-famous statement: 'The fight is here. I need ammunition, not a ride.' This declaration hinted at a significant strength of character that would become apparent as the war unfolded. His words united a nation, inspiring both his people and his international allies to support Ukraine's struggle for independence and sovereignty. This strength was also evident on 2 March 2025 when Zelenskyy sat in the oval office and stood his ground while the world watched. Despite the personal costs, his resilience signalled his commitment to lead the defence of Ukraine, boosting morale among soldiers and civilians alike.

No one is going to give you permission to step up your leadership, so it is about having the courage to own your space. This means at times you may have to have conversations that are not popular and which require a certain degree of tough-mindedness. Humans are attracted to strength. People respect a leader who is strong, has a voice and will stand up for their beliefs. Teams need to see that the boss is capable and effective and has a winning track record. They feel safer with a boss who will stand up to bullies and address dysfunctional or unhelpful behaviours. This attribute needs to be balanced with being open and curious; otherwise, a leader might be perceived to be rigid, arrogant and inflexible. It is a fine line, because they need to be strong enough to be comfortable with discomfort, put courage over comfort and swim against the current when necessary.

You get what you tolerate

Some would say, 'If you allow it, you teach it,' or 'You get what you tolerate.' Leaders are not just role models and yardsticks of standards but also gate-keepers of behaviour. If you don't set the tone, no one else will. Walk past a problem repeatedly and you are part of the problem. Know what high expectations look and sound like; otherwise, you will end up in a culture of mediocrity. Develop a level of concern and a sense of urgency around what is important. You are not weak because you are calm when someone else is aggressive, but being calm does not have to mean you are a doormat. There is no room for disrespectful or aggressive behaviour from adults. You are not able to fix or carry everything, so sometimes you have to take a stand and say, 'This issue is important to me too, but I can't help you while you are being disrespectful – once you calm down, I can help you.'

Put courage over comfort

In leadership there will be many times when you will need to draw on your courage to put courage over comfort or safety over politeness. This can come with a cost or a personal wound. The following are examples of the costs of leadership:

- You will be watched, praised or judged and not always understood and will not always be able to defend yourself.
- You will have to have hard conversations with people you like and consider to be your friends.
- You may be lonely at times, as you can't share everything always.
- You can't please everyone, despite your evidence-based decisions.
- You may feel wounded after taking on a less scrupulous boss.

Strength incorporates interpersonal abilities

A study by Smith and Jones (2021) involving over 300 corporate teams suggests that leadership strength is multifaceted, with both cognitive strengths and interpersonal strengths. The research also highlights that adaptability and a high level of self-awareness are evident in strong leadership, with leaders attuned to their own and others' emotions achieving higher levels of team success. They recommend that leadership programs focus on emotional and interpersonal abilities, not just the technical elements, reinforcing the concept that leadership strength is critical to organisational success.

Survey your strengths

Take a strengths survey such as VIA, available free on the internet (https://www.viacharacter.org). Ask team members to talk about what they enjoy doing and are good at. What would they like to learn in the future and master, to sharpen their expertise? Although there is an argument for every senior member of the leadership team to learn a broad range of skills, because interleaving skills is a way to raise performance and innovation, the neuroscience would also support the notion of everyone being matched to their strengths and passions. We are usually good at what we like doing.

Takeaways

- A leader is praised or blamed, never fully understood.
- A leader gets what they tolerate.
- If the leader is not setting the standard and tone, no one else will.
- Leadership strength is multifaceted and incorporates not only the technical skills but also interpersonal capabilities.
- No one is going to give you permission to step up your leadership; you have to own your space.
- Intervene early and informally as the first step to changing behaviour.
- Leaders can't avoid the hard conversations about serial dysfunction or repeated unhelpful behaviour.
- Walk past repeated dysfunctional behaviour and you are part of the problem.

Reflection and journaling

- What ideas emerged?
- What are your insights and learnings?
- What are your challenges?
- What was confirming?
- What is now clearer for you?
- What will you now do differently?
- What is the one most important thing you will do next?

LEADERSHIP ATTRIBUTE 4: CLARITY

'Your time is limited so don't waste it living someone else's life. Don't be trapped by dogma, which is living with the result of other people's thinking. Don't let the noise of others' opinions drown out your own inner voice.'

Steve Jobs

Seek clarity not certainty

If you have clarity around your purpose, boundaries and standards, the work will be much easier. Clarity is about clear expectations, consistent behaviours, a sense of certainty, using a common language, clear roles and expected results, and line of sight. Line of sight is an essential element of clarity, as it is when you can see clear priorities reflected throughout the school such as in the foyer, on the classroom walls, in student book work, in conversation, on school signage and in the principal's newsletter. In other words, there is clarity around what is important at the school. Setting expectations has a powerful impact. When we state our expectations, others will often live up to those expectations. Our high expectations can lead to higher performance. This is called the Pygmalion effect. Leaders can communicate their clear expectations so that others have a goal to work up to. Research suggests that clarity in leadership is essential for fostering trust, improving team performance, and ensuring that goals are met (Kellerman, 2012). There has never been a time when clarity has been so important to the success of our leadership, as we live in the age of ambiguity where nothing is certain or black and white.

Be mindful that you can't promise certainty but you can ensure clarity. A sense of certainty, consistency and clarity is a strong theme in motivational theory. This is because the brain thinks in expectation and attempts to recognise patterns to predict the future. New information is connected with existing wiring to save brain fuel and make meaning of the information coming in. Producing order and consistency in the workplace to improve certainty and clarity is therefore calming for team members. Surprises and change may trigger the brain into a nonconscious threat response, as it poses a risk to our sense of control and disrupts the safe feeling that certainty brings (Gordon, 2020). Many teachers reported that they are often change-fatigued and indicated that they are looking for consistency of purpose and practice. One teacher stated that when her principal changes the goal posts, it is very unsettling for her. This presents a problem, as sometimes a leader needs to remain adaptable and flexible to change course as new information comes in. What is important to the comfort levels of the individual may not be important for school progress.

Communication around decision-making processes will set a sound foundation for establishing a sense of clarity. Leaders must gain clarity in their decision-making and communication channels if they are to navigate their way through change. The team needs to understand how and why decisions are being made. A clear vision allows leaders to make informed decisions, set expectations, and communicate strategies effectively, aligning team members with organisational objectives (Northouse, 2018). Furthermore, leaders who exhibit clarity are better able to resolve conflicts and navigate complex challenges, creating a more collaborative and productive work environment (Goleman, 2013). If you have not agreed on what high performance is, then when you see poor performance you will not have clarity around how to respond. Effective communication, which is a cornerstone of clarity, is linked to higher employee satisfaction and retention (Bennis, 2009).

Be clear about who you are

Clarity and consistency are also knowing who you are and how you want to be seen by others. Who you are is how you lead. Composure and strength build influence. Troy Barath is a school principal. I was inspired by the way he consistently and professionally approached his interactions with others. It was evident that he had a strong sense of who he was and how he wanted to turn up. His interpersonals, interactions and decisions were all anchored into his concept of leadership. Troy is known in his community for his tradition of gifting a tie to each student in his school as they graduate, as a symbol of what they have learnt on their school journey. He wears a different tie to school each day and then keeps them for graduation day. The ties are all different, some of vibrant colour, some traditional, and others decorated in a theme. His gesture is about giving a little of himself to his students as they leave his care. When I asked Troy to tell me about what this meant for him, this was his story:

I am a firm believer in constant and gentle, for a positive impact leading to long-term change, like water on rock. Having the opportunity to be a reliable, calm certainty that provides support while setting expectations in students' lives is a privilege that I take very seriously. I spend a lot of time working with students in groups and individually to develop their resilience, positive self-talk and self-reflection. I make the conscious decision to prioritise people over paperwork because that is where my impact is the greatest. Giving the ties is a way that I can give a little piece of me, not to remember me but, I hope, to remember those expectations and those ways of working that I think are the keys to being a strong, good human being. My graduation speech to the full school community is a key part of that process:

Good evening, parents, staff and students.

Tonight, as you walk onto the stage to receive your graduation certificate, I want you to make sure you smile for your photo, hold on to the moment and capture it in your memory. It is a moment in time that I would like you to remember, so I am going to give you a gift that will help.

It's not a surprise. Most of you know what it is. But first there are some rules that go with the gift I am giving you.

1. *Don't waste it by throwing it away.*
2. *Don't hurt anyone with it.*
3. *Once you take the gift, it is yours. You can choose to do something creative with it, you can help people with it, you can give it to someone, but it is yours to choose to do what you will with it.*

I have given you each one of the ties I have worn to school this year. There are parallels between the gift I am giving you and the amazing gift of life that you have already been given. You don't get to choose your tie. And in life, you don't get to choose if you are naturally good at sport or maths. You don't get to choose if your family is rich or poor. You don't get to choose if you are tall or short or if you go bald or have lots of hair. But you do get to choose a whole lot of things: you get to choose your attitude every day, you get to choose to study or not, you get to choose whether you make a situation better or worse, you get to choose how you affect others by being a friend or not. Those decisions are yours to make each and every day from now on as you head into high school and the start of your young adult lives.

So, I want to go back to those three rules that relate to your new tie and the rest of your life:

1. *Don't throw it away – do something great with it.*
2. *Don't hurt anyone with it – and if you do, own it and apologise.*
3. *This is your gift – be creative, be adventurous, be safe and just like my ties – be awesome!*

Finally, go out into the world, make new friends and have new experiences but never forget where you came from, who you are and that you have people who care about you – do your best, be your best, make your school, your families and, most importantly, yourselves proud.

Troy is inspirational. I have no doubt that every child who receives a tie is not only going to remember that moment but will reflect on the message as a metaphor for how to live their life. This is: work with what you have, learn and improve, don't waste opportunities, be kind to others and choose your own direction to do something worthy with who you are.

Leadership influence is about giving a little of yourself for others to carry. Troy has created many leadership influence moments. He leads from the heart through connection, from the gut, showing his vulnerability and protective approach, and from the head through his deep reflection about the life message he wants to project. To this day, Troy has given away thousands of ties.

See what others don't see

Schools are places of complexity and uncertainty. Being able to make decisions in an ambiguous context takes perspective. Perspective in regard to clarity refers to our ability to make meaning of situations, to cut through the noise, to see the grey, to find the real issues, to perceive the context, to understand the complexities, to be proactive and responsive in the confusion. Don't be trapped by living with the result of other people's opinions. Taking the time to pick up the cues, to reflect on what is coming and preparing for it, is about perspective. It allows us to be proactive, to look around corners for what might be coming.

Being able to tolerate paradoxes and ambiguity involves being able to see the grey. Black-and-white thinking will let you down as a leader. Most situations are not win/lose or right/wrong. Table 14 profiles the paradox of leadership to help leaders reflect on the complexity of the leadership experience.

One fact or truth	Its opposing tension
Accountable for everything	And in control of nothing but your own behaviour
Seeking equity	At the expense of excellence
Rights of individuals	Versus those of the team
The rules call for policy adherence	While the heart speaks of compromise and compassion
The pressures of being loyal to peers	Versus telling the truth in the interests of justice
Work responsibility	Family life balance
Running a tight ship	Versus generating creativity and risk-taking
Showing strength and ownership	But wanting people to offer their ideas
The need to put on a corporate face, be calm and in control	The need to show your vulnerability to be open and real
You want to do it yourself to do it right	But you can't do it all so you have to let go
Being seen as a clear leader	But sharing your leadership
Leading a future-orientated vision	While managing the reality of events
Sustaining your own wellbeing	Being everything to everyone

One fact or truth	Its opposing tension
Making the right decisions	Versus being popular
Maintaining consistency and routine to reduce stress levels in teams	Versus changing course to adapt to new information coming in as something is implemented

Table 14: Paradox in leadership

Know the hidden rules

Another important element of perspective is understanding that social interactions are governed by hidden rules, unspoken norms and biases that differ significantly across socioeconomic groups. Recognising these rules allows you to see what others can't see.

Dr Ruby Payne (2005) has written extensively on this topic, particularly on the unseen codes of conduct that shape how people in poverty, the middle class, and the wealthy interact with the world. In generational poverty, relationships and entertainment are central. Survival often depends on personal alliances, and the ability to physically defend oneself, or have someone else do it, is seen as essential. Conflict is often managed through action rather than language, as verbal skills may be underdeveloped or disrespected. Humour tends to be loud and spontaneous, with fewer filters, and focused on the personal detail. Education is valued but not viewed as a reality. Food is valued for quantity.

In the middle class, work, achievement and self-sufficiency are prized. Here, words are tools for negotiation and problem-solving. Conflict is expected to be handled through calm discussion, and success is measured by individual accomplishments. Education is viewed as a pathway to stability and advancement. Humour tends to be about situations and experiences and very personal sensitive matters are politely avoided. Food is valued for quality.

In wealthy circles, the emphasis is on financial, social and political influence. Global thinking shapes their world view, and strategic relationships are cultivated through networking for long-term gain. Polished manners and formal etiquette protocols are observed, discreet humour is valued, and social norms are often enforced subtly but rigidly. Food is prized for presentation and for the famous chef associated with its preparation.

It is not only our financial status that can shape hidden rules. Associate Professor Yolanda Ruiz Scarfuto Sealy's concept of the 'Archaeology of Self' is about digging through one's personal and collective experiences, which have been shaped by history, trauma, race, socio-political status, and colonialism, to uncover deeply embedded values, beliefs, assumptions and identities. She highlights that we need to know what we bring to the table before we can lead others, especially with marginal groups. Acknowledging the limitations of one's own viewpoint, recognising personal bias, and embracing learning for continuous growth takes deep sustained reflection on who we are and how this affects our behaviour.

As leaders, educators or influencers, being socially and culturally attuned to these hidden rules allows us to lead with perspective, providing greater clarity, empathy and effectiveness across diverse contexts.

Slow decision-making down

Sometimes we see effective leaders as decisive people who can make quick decisions. When we make quick decisions, our brain will often take the path of least resistance and connect to the neural wiring that represents the things we already know well. This may serve us well in an emergency, but at times our thinking needs to slow down to pose questions to give our brain the opportunity over time to rewire and reflect. Decisions that appear to be simple may not be. Taking the time to reduce cognitive bias and make more accurate improved decisions that address the root cause or real issues will save time in the long term. Senge (2000, pp. 77–78) points out that we grow skilled at moving from one problem or crisis to another instead of slowing down and finding ways to prevent them.

> *'If I had eight hours to chop down a tree,*
> *I'd spend six hours sharpening the axe.'*
> Abraham Lincoln

Mitigate cognitive bias

All staff won't always agree with a decision but if they know how and why the decision was made they are more likely to accept that decision.

Additionally, if people have been part of a collaborative decision-making process, they are more likely to understand and own the decision. As they say, you don't tear down what you have come to build together. Having a decision-making process and model will provide clarity and some sense of control in an uncertain situation.

Table 15 outlines a way to make decisions that maximise ownership and minimise cognitive bias by first looking through ten windows. The first window refers to what we know. We may be a genius in our own head, but if we make all our decisions based on that assumption, our view may be too narrow. Drawing on research and the collective expertise in the group will provide a more comprehensive perspective. The sum of the team's expertise can outweigh individual intelligence (Surowiecki, 2004, pp. xii–xiv). Additionally, exploring the mental models of the team will assist in moving towards clarity and collective understanding because our deeply held beliefs shape how we see the world and impact our thinking. A variety of mental models about a heartfelt issue can make decision-making difficult because beliefs and biases exist below the level of conscious awareness, and are often untested and unexamined (Senge, 2000, p. 67). Calling the elephants in the room, mining for reasons for resistance, lowering anxiety and mitigating cognitive bias are tools for the effective school leader. Before you make decisions, looking through the ten windows shown in Table 15 will help establish clarity, ownership and trust.

1	What you know	What is in your head?
2	World's best practice	Who is doing it well?
3	Pooled team expertise	Draw out the collective expertise but be aware of 'groupthink'.
4	Impact	Identify the consequences of all options being considered. What is the impact on people?
5	World views	Mine for beliefs and assumptions, because these will impact on thinking. What is your intuition saying?
6	Internal data	Check your data.

7	Purpose	What outcome do you want? Keep the why in mind.
8	Research	What does the research say?
9	Problem of practice (root cause)	Identify the factors that inhibit and slow down change.
10	Enablers of practice	Identify the factors that amplify and speed up change.

Table 15: The ten windows

The ten windows allow us to slow down our decision-making to consider mental models and intuition associated with brain one, impacts on how people feel and our moral purpose associated with brain two, and qualitative and quantitative data and research associated with brain three.

Decision-making noise

In their book *Noise: A Flaw in Human Judgment,* Kahneman et al. (2021) explore how inconsistent human judgments impact decision-making. They point out that noise differs from bias in that it is the unwanted variability in human judgment. The book highlights that people make different decisions in very similar scenarios, leading to costly errors, potential unfairness and inconsistency. Unlike bias, which causes a distortion of thinking in one direction, noise is random and unpredictable. In education, consequences in behaviour management decisions must be contextual (and so they should), but I wonder how much noise would be found in similar situations in different schools. I also wonder if different teachers have different rules from one classroom to the next and what effect the level of noise has on the way students view fairness.

Anchor into a decision-making framework

Table 16 outlines a simple decision-making model that will help clarify the why, how and what of decision-making. People don't have to agree with a decision you have made as a leader of a team but they do need to understand the why, what and how if you want to bring them along with you. The key is working out together what a strategic, tactical and operational decision is. It works well if most decisions are Mode 2, where the senior leadership team consult all staff. As the highest accountable officer, the principal needs to make policy decisions at times.

Mode	Who makes the decision	Type of decision
1	Autocratic: Principal decision	Strategic decision
2	Consultative: Team decision	Tactical decision
3	Inclusive: All staff decision	Operational decision

Table 16: A decision-making model

The blue line

The blue line concept was introduced in the 2013 book *The Blue Line Imperative: A Radical New Approach to Value-Based Leadership* by Kevin Kaiser and S. David Young. It has been modified by later consultants to establish behaviour expectations. If you have had previous discussions about clear expectations, when things go pear-shaped it is easier to sort them out because you have something solid to anchor into, such as agreed roles and behaviours. High-performance teams discuss behaviours that reflect the professionalism and ethics of the team and the behaviours that don't align with the values of the organisation. Work with your team to articulate and record what behaviours you want to see above the blue line and what behaviours you don't want to see below the blue line. So that this important work is not taken personally, it can be beneficial to profile the personalities and strengths of the team first and then the collective discussion can refer to the behaviours that are typical of the personality types rather than the individual. Figure 7 illustrates the blue line.

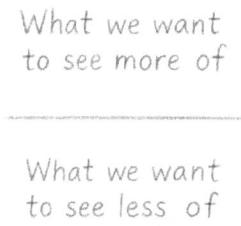

Figure 7: The blue line activity

Takeaways

- For clarity, look outside your own head when making decisions to mitigate cognitive bias.
- Schools with a strong sense of clarity have a clear line of sight.
- Composure and strength build influence.
- Clarity, consistency and certainty make humans feel safe.
- If you change the goal posts, make sure you explain the why.
- Clarify roles and expectations so that everyone knows what they should be spending their time on.
- Talk through professional behaviours you want to see more of and less of so that when you do see poor performance you can address it more easily.
- Leadership influence is about giving a little of yourself away.
- Leaders have a clear view about who they are, their impact and how they want to turn up.
- There is a degree of noise in decision-making from one person to another.
- Mitigate cognitive bias in decision-making.

Reflection and journaling

- What ideas emerged?
- What are your insights and learnings?
- What are your challenges?
- What was confirming?
- What is now clearer for you?
- What will you now do differently?
- What is the one most important thing you will do next?

LEADERSHIP ATTRIBUTE 5: POSITIVITY

'People get hired on their skill and fired on their attitude.'
Simon Sinek

Look for the good and see the opportunities

A leader who is positive promotes the language of hope. They look for the good and see opportunities. Other behaviours that are captured in this category are: having a positive, helpful attitude, being solution-focused, showing passion for the work and people, using positive framing, applying humour to diffuse tension, expressing gratitude and optimism, bringing joy into the work and celebrating team success. Positive mindsets, optimistic language and joyful cultures, as evident in the way staff and students interact with one another, tend to set off the release of dopamine, oxytocin and serotonin, forming the conditions for the brain states that rewire and reinforce positive behaviour. A positive mindset is a choice.

I was reminded of this fact while working with a remote school on an island off the top end of Australia. Over three visits, I came to know the leadership team well. The island itself was a peaceful setting, the indigenous community warm and welcoming, but the working conditions were undeniably tough.

What stood out to me wasn't the isolation or the challenges – it was the executive principal, Terry Byrne, and her remarkable team. Despite limited resources, long hours, and complex student needs, their mindset remained unfailingly positive. Their commitment to their students, to each other, and to the wider community radiated through every conversation and interaction. In fact, their optimism and unity eclipsed many urban schools with far more comforts and far fewer hurdles. That experience crystallised something for me: **mindset is a choice**. That's the real magic of school leadership influence: bringing the community along with you. Terry's team had no hint of a 'them and us' attitude. When a school team is aligned in belief, respect and purpose, and shows a desire to continue to grow and learn, there's no limit to what can be achieved together.

Sometimes in leadership we need to show confidence and strength outwardly, but inside feel uncertain and anxious. Your head is telling you to put on a brave face, your heart is reminding you to be kind, while your gut is trying to protect you by playing small. Be aware when your head, heart and gut are out of sync and align them, as that will serve you best.

We learn and think more rationally in a positive emotional state creating positive neural traits (Hanson & Mendius, 2009). Deal and Peterson (2016, p. 5) argue that many 'schools are in danger of losing the notion of schools as joyful places of promise and hope and becoming more like factories', missing key components of what a well-educated person needs to grow.

When conditions are challenging and uncertain, providing hope for the team can inspire them to take the path they can't see (Day, 2015). The tone and disposition of the leader can make a significant positive impact on the team's motivation levels and mood. Mood is contagious, as the brain picks up tonal and interpersonal cues (Boyatzis, 2012) directly impacting the emotion of the listener. Gordon (2022) argues that tonality is around 50 per cent of what others will detect and respond to when interacting as opposed to 10 per cent impact from the words used. Inspiring leaders show enthusiasm and excitement and that passion indicates to the team that the leader has a personal conviction regarding the work they are doing together (Kouzes & Posner, 1990).

Gratitude and optimism reset chronic negativity

We have a social brain, and the brain tips to the negative, so it is easy to fall into the complaining trap. Small comments complaining about people or the school can slowly strengthen neural pathways over time, changing how we think (Belynder, 2024). The neuroplastic nature of the brain is responding to the repeated habitual thinking, rewiring circuits based on how we feel, evolving into a pessimistic mindset. Negativity triggers cortisol, which can also weaken the immune system, increase anxiety, and raise blood pressure. Repeated negative thinking reinforces negative neural pathways and makes them more likely to be repeated the next day. Negative neural states wire negative neural traits.

David Manttan is a former school principal who had a reputation for establishing positive school cultures way before textbooks talked about the benefits of positive psychology. During his tenure as a principal, Dave encountered schools where the prevailing culture involved managing students through negative reinforcement and critical communication among staff members. When I asked Dave how he shifted the school's culture towards one characterised by positive and constructive interactions, he explained that cultural transformation is one of the most challenging tasks, as it is deeply rooted in the daily conversations that reflect the established norms and practices. New staff members often become assimilated into this culture through the behaviours and dialogues of their colleagues, frequently without realising its impact on students.

Recognising that teachers are inherently motivated to benefit children, Dave role-modelled consistent 'corridor conversations' that emphasised two or three key desired behaviours. These were integrated into his casual, incidental discussions with individual staff members throughout the school. He ensured that his actions and interactions with students exemplified the desired behaviours. Formal conversations at school assemblies were utilised to reinforce and reward these behaviours among students.

To monitor the progress of this cultural change, Dave paid attention to informal staff conversations. He noticed that the narrative shifted from comments like 'John is still calling others names like his brother did' to observations such as 'I saw John working with Letia and thanking her for her help'. Over a period of one to two years, these strategies significantly contributed to creating a welcoming environment for both students and staff, where success was consistently celebrated.

Your response can be part of the problem

Another pivotal moment in my leadership journey in regard to positivity also involved Dave. He always demonstrated a calm, honest, encouraging and mild-mannered demeanour which inspired trust from others. He was visiting my school one day and I was a little anxious about something that had gone pear-shaped; as the accountable officer, I didn't want to disappoint him or be seen to be incompetent in his eyes. I explained the situation and how I managed it, providing detail. I talked about how I re-established relationships and apologised for getting it wrong. He listened without interrupting and then said, 'That could have happened to anyone, Judi. The way you have responded and handled the situation is what is important.'

Adults are the first to apologise, the first to reconnect and restore the relationship. I realise now that our response to events can sometimes be part of the problem and it can make all the difference. To this day, I can't remember what went wrong that week, but I do remember Dave's response. I was delighted that Dave didn't judge me when I was feeling vulnerable, and that taught me a lot about leadership. It encouraged me to be more open and honest rather than project my fears and ego. Dave's success in schools led to a long career in leadership positions at executive level where his mentoring benefited hundreds of principals. He is currently working as an educational consultant.

A negative mindset can be interrupted and reset by focusing on gratitude (Belynder, 2024). Rather than allowing your brain to default to autopilot, direct your focus on the things you are grateful for, switching to an optimistic mindset to rewire your neutral pathways for improved wellbeing. Your relationships will also benefit, because people prefer to be around positive people rather than critical ones. Ways you can express gratitude include telling someone how much you appreciate them: 'I could not have done this without you.' Write handwritten thank you notes. Before you go to sleep, think of three things you are grateful for. When things get tricky, look for the bright side: the learning, the opportunity or the beauty.

Leaders use the language of hope

Nothing good comes from spreading messages of fear or criticising colleagues, because what you tell one person will be repeated to others. I had the pleasure of hearing Barack Obama, former President of the United States, speak live in Melbourne on the subject of leadership influence. He stated that, as a leader, it is easy to tell stories that incite fear, and much more difficult to tell stories of hope. He believes that it is very important for a leader to unite people towards a common goal and give them hope. He models optimism in his speeches, some of which are quoted below:

> *'We are the change that we seek.'*
> Keynote address at the Democratic National Convention in Denver, Colorado, 2008.

> *'The future rewards those who press on.'*
> Remarks at the National Governors Association Winter Meeting, 2011.

> *'Yes, we can.'*
> Victory speech after winning the Iowa caucus, 2008.

> *'In the face of impossible odds, people who love their country can change it.'*
> Victory speech after winning the Iowa caucus, 2008.

> *'We are the ones we've been waiting for. We are the change that we seek.'*
> At a campaign rally in Richmond, Virginia, 2008.

> *'Hope is what gives us the strength to keep going.'*
> During a speech in Chicago, 2010.

> *'We may not get there in one year or even one term, but we can get there.'*
> During his campaign for the presidency in New Hampshire, 2008.

The power of the attachment emotions

The attachment emotions of trust, love, joy, hope, curiosity and gratefulness build neural architecture. The survival emotions of disgust, anger, distrust, shame and sadness inhibit synaptic growth. Associate Professor Julie Jhun and her dynamic team run an exceptional leadership course for aspiring and sitting school principals at California State University, Dominguez Hills. In California, school principals are required to complete a preliminary licensure program to be eligible to become a school administrator. Julie is an insightful speaker on school leadership, so I asked her to share a pivotal leadership moment. She told me about a six-year-old student who had tested her patience every day during her first year of teaching. He had a great deal of anger for a young child, and she said, 'His continuous rebellious outbursts defeated me. When my principal shared with me that Devin [not his real name] was born prematurely, was a drug baby and had spent the first two years of his life in an incubator, I was overwhelmed with compassion.' She said love lies at the heart of leadership. 'I understood Devin's anger and my patience was fully renewed. Even a six-year-old could see through my disingenuity. It was not until I shifted my own mindset and beliefs about Devin that he began to respond through a lens of love.'

Dopamine gives us an achievement bias

We get a shot of dopamine when we feel good. We feel good when we achieve something, when we cross something off our to-do list, when we win, or when we have a glass of wine. Dopamine gives us an achievement bias in that if we do something that makes us feel good, we are more likely to do it again. Michael Merzenich, an American neurophysiologist, and his colleagues studied mice, stimulating particular neural pathways associated with their dopamine and acetylcholine circuits. As these neurons fired repeatedly, they were amplified, rewiring the cortical maps. When a sound was associated with the neural circuits and a dopamine hit, the mouse's brain became highly sensitive and aroused to that sound and similar sounds. In fact, the mouse became better at discriminating sounds associated with the original sound but it partially lost its ability to process other sound frequencies (Bao et al., 2001; Froemke et al., 2007). If this neuroplastic rewiring can be applied to the human brain, it may imply that passion reshapes and amplifies the neural networks into an expertise it is associated with. The release of dopamine in our reward centres not only means that we are more likely to repeat something that feels good, but it also makes the associated skill it has been paired with more efficient.

There is much research to show that positivity also benefits team performance and wellbeing. In a paper by Horwitch and Chipple-Callahan (2016), Associate Professor Jennifer Thompson from the Chicago School of Psychology carried out an empirical study showing that when people have positive environments, they are more creative and productive. Negative workplaces and attitudes shut down the brain in that they inhibit people's problem-solving skills and narrow their thinking. Positive psychology researchers generally agree that optimistic people are better able to deal with adversity and are more satisfied in their jobs (Gordon, 2020). The arousal of positive emotions stimulates the parasympathetic nervous system, which is associated with neurogenesis, the release of dopamine, a sense of wellbeing, group mood and innovation. Thus, an important technique of a school leader is the ability to shift and change their internal mental state, especially given that the brain has four times more neural networks for negative feelings than positive feelings.

Dopamine-makers make us feel good

We can do things to make us feel good to stimulate a more positive mood. These are ways you can produce a shot of dopamine:

- Hum and listen to upbeat music
- Eat a little chocolate
- Cross off tasks on a to-do list
- Get something done
- Finish something
- Cuddle a fluffy bundle of cuteness
- Pick wild flowers
- List what you are grateful for
- Have a giggle with a friend
- Visualise your best self
- Random acts of kindness.

Dopamine-boosters and cortisol-makers

The words we use can have a negative or a positive impact and can potentially rewire our brain for improved wellbeing and performance through coaching. Some words and behaviours create cortisol (stress hormone) and others create dopamine, serotonin and oxytocin. To show this in a simple way, Table 17 lists cortisol-makers and dopamine-boosters.

We are much more able to learn and focus when we are not stressed and are curious and content (Willis, 2020). A positive mindset, a non-judgmental setting and encouragement provide the best conditions for trust and learning to flourish.

Cortisol-makers	Dopamine-boosters
Unhappy	Joyful
Tell	Ask
Distracted	Focused
Rattled	Calm
Rushed	Relaxed
Bullied	Kind
Blame	Pride
Confusion	Clarity
Correct	Praise
Unfair	Fair
Isolated	Connected
Trapped	Free
Make	Invite
Disgust	Awe

Table 17: Dopamine boosters

Learn positive framing

The way we phrase what we want to say will have an impact on our degree of influence. A leader's words have power. Learning to choose words carefully for impact can be a simple tool. Table 18 shows how terms can be reframed to have a positive impact.

Tattletale	Seeks justice, respectful of rules
Bossy	Has clarity, strength of character
Rebellious	Finding their way
Attention-seeking	Seeks connection
Fussy	Has high standards and attention to detail
Defiant	Determined, brave, holding their ground
Fearful	Cautious, careful

Table 18: Positive framing

Motivational positive response model

Teaching students and teachers to communicate with each other in a positively responsive way can improve the workplace culture of the school. The schools that are using the tool below report improved staff morale and student wellbeing. Figure 8 illustrates the four brain states in a team when interacting:

- **Passive agitate state:** People tend to avoid, play small and go into freeze-or-flight mode. 'I hate Mondays.'
- **Passive contribute state:** People show a lack of energy in their response but move through the motions. 'Morning.'
- **Active agitate state:** People are stressed and show their frustration. 'I would rather be anywhere else.'
- **Active contribute state:** People invest energy in the way they respond. 'Hi, Jane, I am glad I ran into you. How was your weekend? I heard you won your tennis match.'

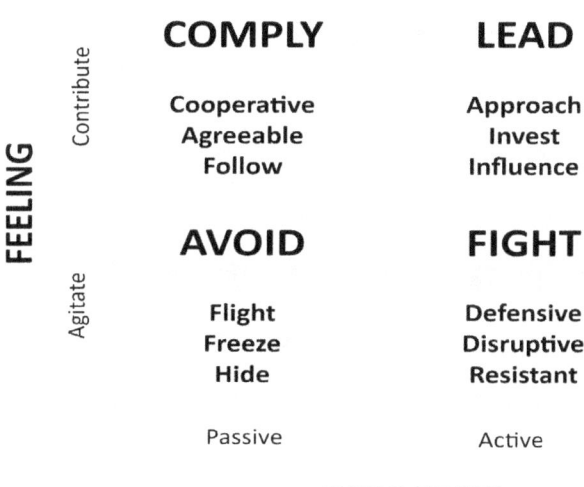

Figure 8: Motivation response model

From drama to agency

Humans tend to like drama when things get exciting, but being a drama queen is not helpful to a leadership approach in the workplace. The Okojo

Protocol is an excellent tool to help people understand what role they are playing in the drama. Our mindset sets our manner. The Okojo Protocol helps identify what our starting gate looks like and is shown in Figure 9 and Table 19.

The Okojo Protocol (Newman, 2010) was created during my master's research and is informed by the Drama Triangle by Rodolph B. Karpman (1968); Model 1 and 2 by Argris and Schon (1974); the Art of the Question by Goldberg (1998); and the Fixed and Growth Mindset by Carol Dweck (2006) – and refined over many years of observing behaviour.

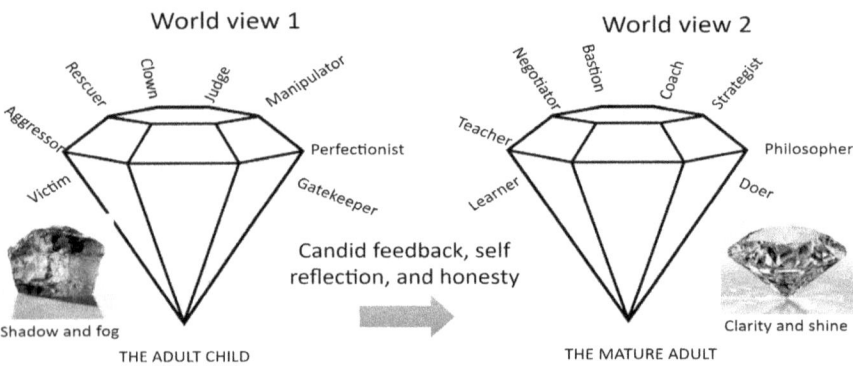

Figure 9: The Okojo Protocol

World view 1	World view 2
Agitate state	Contribute state
Reactive	Proactive
Closed to learning and feedback	Open to learning and feedback
Low self-awareness	High self-awareness
Blind to their impact on others	Aware of their impact on others
Finding blame or fault	Being accountable and taking ownership
A know-it-all attitude	What am I missing here?
Self-focused and lives in their head	Sees the grey and seeks perspective

Table 19: Moving from world view 1 to 2

Mindset roles

We all play roles, as shown in Table 20. The Okojo Protocol has eight pairs of roles. On a daily basis we can move from one to another. However, we aim to be in world view 2 most of the time. To move into world view 2 as a mature adult we must be highly self-reflective, seek feedback from others, be honest with ourselves and know our starting gate. Your starting gate is what you tend to default to.

World view 1	World view 2
Victim	**Learner**
'It's all about me. It's everybody else's fault.'	*'What can I learn from this?'*
Suffer from being problem-focused. Done to by others.	Seek to find the new learning. Problem-solve themselves.
Aggressor	**Teacher**
'I am angry and want control.'	*'I can advise to help.'*
On the attack. Combative, defensive, competitive and intimidating. Do to others. Listen to defend their ground.	Able to pass on and share knowledge and skills, assertive to educate, instruct and engage as expert. Listen to learn.
Rescuer	**Negotiator**
'I want to save them and be popular.'	*'I will negotiate the options.'*
Help and assist by doing it for them. Deny others the learning, creating dependence.	Solution-oriented. Problem-solver. Show them how to do it for themselves.
Manipulator	**Strategist**
'I want to exert my influence for my own advantage.'	*'I want to influence for the benefit of all.'*
Not transparent. Have ulterior motives and unfair influence. Cunning. Game players.	Clever use of resources to gain influence. No games.

World view 1	World view 2
Judge 'My view is the most likely right.' Assess from own point of view and make assumptions. Opinionated. Not always evidence-based. Look for fault without understanding context and radiate blame vibes. Knower. Judgmental.	**Coach** 'I will question to seek all the information.' Unlock a person's potential. Ask questions and tap into expertise. Listen for understanding of context. Enquirer.
Perfectionist 'If it is not perfect, it is a failure.' See everything in black and white. Put pressure on self. Rigid. Bound to be disappointed. Give off an air of invincibility.	**Philosopher** 'I seek to provide insight and perspective.' Calm, reflective. See the grey. Identify truth and underlying premises. Non-judgmental. Wise.
Clown 'I will entertain myself.' I don't care enough to take it seriously. Sarcastic. Nothing will touch me. What can I say to stir the pot?	**Bastion** 'I will lift others up.' Sentinel, stronghold, rock, resilient, centred, beacon of positivity. What can I say to move the situation or person forward?
Gate-keeper 'I am the keeper of the knowledge.' When threatened, stone wall. Listen to defend not to learn. Possibilities seen as limited. Protective. Find blockers. Complicate things. Procrastinator. Want all the details before they move on an idea.	**Doer** 'I want to get what matters done.' See the possibilities. Take responsibility for action. Look for enablers. Make the complicated simple. Do not procrastinate.

Table 20: The mindset roles

In contribute state they are the adult. They are confident and mature enough to be the first to apologise, reconnect and restore the relationship. They can take their ego out. They know their impact on others and they aim to be in world view 2 despite the stress and pressure of the day. When stressed, human beings often resort to our more primitive behaviours as our thinking narrows when the brain is under threat. What is your starting gate?

Takeaways

- An influential leader talks the language of hope.
- We learn and think more rationally in a positive emotional state.
- The mood of the leader is contagious.
- When conditions are challenging, providing hope can inspire others to take a path they cannot see.
- Tone is 50 per cent of your impact.
- Gratitude and optimism reset automatic negative thinking.
- Positive workplaces are linked to increased creativity and higher performance.
- Communicate in an active-contribute style to enhance impact.
- Adopt some dopamine hits throughout your day.
- Know your starting gate for the mindset roles you play.

Reflection and journaling

- What ideas emerged?
- What are your insights and learnings?
- What are your challenges?
- What was confirming?
- What is now clearer for you?
- What will you now do differently?
- What is the one most important thing you will do next?

LEADERSHIP ATTRIBUTE 6: CONNECTEDNESS

'How you treat one person gets discussed by many.'
Stephen Covey

Show warmth

Connectedness is a strong motivator to engage others. The leadership behaviours that are grouped in this category include showing warmth, providing support, getting to know people beyond their role, putting the human first, being responsive to people's emotional needs, building strong connections for productive relationships, kindness, and developing strong bonds in the group for a sense of belonging to the tribe.

Staff reported that responsiveness was an important element of feeling connected to a leader. They said that it is essential for a school principal to connect in such a way that the team member they are conversing with feels their emotions have been acknowledged as a part of responding to their needs. A degree of empathy is required to be responsive to others (Zaki & Ochsner, 2012). In her thesis, Lambruschini (2016) studied the interpersonal connection that leaders have with others and how this connection can inspire others, finding that leaders had deep connections through communicating on the same wavelength, extending trust in others, paying individuals attention, giving absolute focus and checking in with each other on a personal level. Other studies (such as Steffens & Haslam, 2013) discuss the importance of using the pronoun 'we' rather than 'I' to build connectedness. The use of collective pronouns by the leader can develop trust and contribute to 'in-group' behaviours (Molenberghs et al., 2015) that establish rapport and are conducive to engagement and ownership. All principals in my study showed some evidence of the use of the collective pronouns 'we' and 'our' when they interacted with staff members. They used collective pronouns more than the singular pronouns 'I' and 'you'.

One of the most inspiring leadership moments of former New Zealand Prime Minister Jacinda Ardern illustrated the power of 'we' after the Christchurch mosque attacks on 15 March 2019. She declared, 'They are us,' showing that the Muslim community was an integral part of the New Zealand community. She was shown on the television news report at the time, turning up personally and hugging the Muslim families who had gathered at the site. She said, 'We represent diversity, kindness, compassion, and a home for those who share our values.' She was able to inspire hope and unity when she showed her humanity and connected through her words and touch.

This would support the conclusion that the person-to-person connection signifies inspirational leadership. However, Willink and Babin (2017, p. 277), highlight a caution in relation to a strong connection between leaders and their teams. They agree that the best leaders get to know their people and understand their passions and motivations, but they should not become 'so close that one member of the team becomes more important than another or more important than the mission'.

Warmth and empathy or power and status

In her book *The Silent Language of Leaders*, Carol Kinsey Goman (2011) states that successful leaders will increasingly develop more warmth. She explains that leaders can project warmth and empathy, building trust, as opposed to relationships of power and status concerned with position and authority. At a large coastal private school, principal Kara Krehlik exemplifies a leadership manner that projects warmth and empathy. She is always quick to connect and is curious rather than entitled in her manner. This outstanding school cultivates a nurturing environment where strong, meaningful relationships between students, staff and families are at the heart of everything. With a relentless focus on student success as a brain-wise school, it empowers every girl from Prep to Year 12 to thrive academically, socially and emotionally.

I have worked with Kara many times over the years, and recently when I was working with her team I asked her if the relationship focus was an intentional strategy in her leadership. She said that she has a deep commitment to fostering a culture of connection, confidence and engagement. 'As a relational leader, I recognise that before our students can become confident and clever learners, they must first feel connected.' She explains that when students feel connected, they develop the confidence to interact with one another, engage in their academic pursuits, and explore cocurricular opportunities. 'We begin with connectedness, ensuring that students feel safe, valued, and emotionally engaged before building their confidence to take academic and personal risks, ultimately enabling them to become clever, critical thinkers.'

This belief has shaped Kara's leadership philosophy and underpins the way she engages with the wider school community. This same approach is reflected in Kara's leadership of staff across teaching and non-teaching roles. By prioritising connection and confidence, she creates an environment where her executive team and staff feel empowered to innovate and collaborate. She wants to ensure that every member of the school community feels seen, supported and valued by prioritising a focus on relationships. She points out that this is particularly important for the 100 girls who board at the school.

Show empathy not sympathy

Teachers picked up on the importance of the difference between empathy and sympathy when they saw it expressed by their principal. The word empathy comes from a translation of the German word *Einfühling*, which means 'feeling into'. It is the ability to understand another, by trying to understand what it is like to be in their shoes, and is non-judgmental. Sympathy, on the other hand, buys into the feelings – for example, 'You poor thing' – and can weaken the position of a person who needs to feel strong. It may also sound condescending. Empathy shows you are trying to grasp how the person feels without feeling like the person feels. It expresses support for the person's potential and an acknowledgment of their feelings. Using empathy as opposed to sympathy will be more likely to get people's cooperation and agreement because they feel listened to and understood. Other studies show that it is actually compassion, not empathy, that a leader needs to nurture, pointing out that if someone is too empathetic they may cry with the individual and not be in a position to help them. If the leader's emotional brain is activated, they compromise their ability to utilise their thinking brain, thereby reducing their ability to problem-solve and think logically.

Connect through kindness and encouragement

A school leader has the opportunity to touch the hearts and minds of thousands of young people. Sometimes, your influence may have a lifelong positive benefit, which might not be noticeable at the time. When I met Dave and listened to his story, I could see how connection and encouragement can have lifelong impacts. Dave is a successful author, husband, father and former electrician. He has a master's in educational neuroscience. He is kind, clever and funny. He has written a book called *Living Beyond Limits*. Dave has faced significant challenges, as he experiences a number of neurodiverse conditions. He mentioned to me that he had a hard time at school, so I asked him, if he could give a message to school principals, what would he say?

These are Dave's words:

> *Dear Principals,*
>
> *I know you will be able to assist many young people to excel at learning as part of your important role as an educational leader. Some others, like me, you will just succeed in keeping them turning up. Let me explain. I was 'that kid' who was not getting it. I was 'that kid' who achieved nothing in school, period, but just looked out the window. My performance in class was not only dismal but often disruptive due to my undiagnosed neurodiverse conditions of Tourette's syndrome, Obsessive Compulsive Disorder (OCD), a stutter and Attention Deficit Hyper Disorder (ADHD).*
>
> *Like many neurodiverse kids, I was already 'busy in my head' before the school morning began, adding to my cognitive load. My low self-esteem, my continual illogical anxieties and the fear of standing out or being bullied, made the thought of school a fearful one.*
>
> *OCD for me, is like an incessant sort of mental blackmail. Throughout my school age days, I dealt with a constant stream of uninvited thoughts. I also had rituals that I was compelled to do, in order to lessen the stress. If I didn't submit to a ritual, I thought something bad would happen.*

The uninvited, intrusive thoughts were often religious in nature. For example, I would have to say prayers at night in exactly the right sequence, in order for my parents not to die. I used to have to pray for every plane that flew over so it would not crash. I would hold on desperately, not wanting to ask to go to the toilet, in case I embarrassed myself with my stutter, when asking a question in front of the class. I was always anxious, being hypervigilant and on the defensive for anything that would make me feel worse. This was the 1970s in New Zealand and my conditions and disorders were undiagnosed and misunderstood.

I also have symmetry, where I need things to be even. One day I accidently burnt one hand on the stove and I had to burn the other one, to exactly the same degree or repeat it, until I got it right. It has all the slavery of an addiction with the tyranny of a mental illness but without the dopamine hit!

To this day I still can't step on the cracks in concrete. Add my Tourette's syndrome contribution of involuntary sounds and tics and you can guess I had moments that were hard to bear.

Neuroscience shows us that all experience is learning and in school, a child can come to love learning or find that experience burdensome and oppressive. With kids like me, a lot will depend on the quality of the relationships they have with their teachers. A major key to my later success, and something that has stayed with me all these years, is that particular teachers showed kindness and encouraged me, connecting in a way that inspired me to keep trying.

Despite my parents' industry around finding a diagnosis for my squeaks and tics, I tried a range of medication and treatments, all to fail. In desperation, my parents took me to Auckland Hospital to see a leading professor. After examining me and listening to my story, as I walked out of Ward 12 in 1977, he told my parents, 'Take him home and look after him. He will probably never hold down a job. Occupy him with simple tasks. It would be best to keep him out of the public eye. He won't fit in with general society.' Luckily, they ignored this advice and I went back to school the very next day.

After dropping out of high school in year 9, I was sent to a workshop for the disabled. Later, in that disabled workshop, I met a mentor who unlocked my learning potential, by building on my strengths, allowing me choice and providing encouragement and connection.

So the one thing I want to leave you with is: when a student leaves your school, if all you have managed to do is instil in them a love of learning and helped them to feel a connection of acceptance with others, you will have done them a great service. Encourage teachers to invest in four scoops of support to one scoop of challenge.

Connectedness is essential for brain growth

In 1989 the Romanian dictatorship was overthrown and officials discovered 170,000 children being raised in impoverished institutions. They had survived a lack of love and connection with a loving parent but had severe developmental challenges. The interviews with survivors have been well documented and they talk about groups of babies and toddlers left to their own devices in cots, with food left out on a table and very little connection from any adults.

Researchers funded a study where 68 Romanian children (as many as the budget would stretch to at the time) were placed with loving foster parents (Group A) and 68 stayed in the institution (Group B). The children ranged from six months to three years of age. As part of the study, they also observed a control group (Group C) of children who lived in the local village with their natural families.

Group A made dramatic gains in IQ, attachments, social and emotional development, language and ability to express emotion, but still lagged behind the control group. Those removed before the age of two made the biggest gains, but MRI scans showed that the grey and white matter in the brain was reduced compared to normal children. By the age of eight, their brain scans were looking more like those of the local village children (Kirsten, 2007). This is a shocking example of what happens to the developing brain when it is deprived of basic nutrition and love. More recent brain-scanning shows that emotional and social deprivation results in a reduction in brain volume, changes in the prefrontal cortex, difficulty with working memory, struggles to regulate emotions, higher levels of anxiety, abnormal cortisol patterns stunting growth, language problems, motor control difficulties and cognitive function issues (Nelson et al., 2007; Weir, 2014).

Chronic loneliness shrinks the brain

Dr Julianne Holt-Lunstad from Brigham Young University found that social isolation raised a person's risk of death by 50 per cent, which is very high considering that obesity raised it by 30 per cent. Further studies have shown that the lack of social engagement was shown to be on a par with smoking in shortening the life span. Chronic loneliness in unhappy people shrinks the brain.

See the human

A Gallup *State of the American Workplace* report (Harter, 2024) found that employees who think their leaders care about them as a person beyond their role are more likely to be engaged; 37 per cent of workers strongly agreed that they could approach their managers to ask any question, and 27 per cent of workers strongly agreed that they could talk to their managers about topics outside of work. These findings impact on performance, innovation and the ability of a leader to influence.

Bar-Ilan University in Israel and the University of Michigan found that empathy and kindness are absolutely critical for creating higher levels of psychological safety to foster innovation. People are much more willing to share their ideas and admit their errors in a climate of kindness (Carmeli et al., 2009). Researchers at the University of Delaware also found that a combination of kindness and fairness had a significant impact on performance and wellbeing. When a team perceive that they are valued for their contribution and that the company cares about their wellbeing, they feel a reciprocal obligation and desire to perform at their best. They also reported higher job satisfaction and job retention rates and lower turnover (Rhoades & Eisenberger, 2002).

Remember names

If people know you care, they will try harder. I know this, but I found it hard to remember everyone's name, especially the cleaning staff, who changed often. People thought I had a great memory, but I cheated. I kept an A–Z notebook and recorded the key information about my team so that when I checked in with them I could look it up and be in touch with what was going on for them. I recorded their family names, pets and any big events in their life that they cared to tell me about. I think it is important that when someone has been away ill for two weeks I check in with them on their return to work, and when someone loses a parent, I reach out, no matter how awkward it feels. One of the teachers I interviewed said, 'When you know the principal cares on a personal level, I think professionally you are a lot more motivated – in the end you want to impress them because they are looking after you, they show they care. You want to do the right thing by them, so you bring out your best performance.'

Takeaways

- Our brain evolved to belong to and operate in a social group.
- A degree of empathy boosts connection.
- Kindness boosts innovation.
- Empathy and sympathy have a different impact on the way we connect.
- Compassion may be better than empathy when helping others.
- The interpersonals of leaders can project power and status associated with position and authority, or warmth and empathy associated with trust and rapport.
- Chronic loneliness and disconnection shrink brain matter and are a risk to our wellbeing.
- Some students are resilient; others are fragile. They all can benefit from one scoop of challenge to four scoops of support.
- Use 'we' and 'us', not 'I' and 'me'.
- High expectations have to be upheld in a setting of kindness, love, protection and encouragement.

Reflection and journaling

- What ideas emerged?
- What are your insights and learnings?
- What are your challenges?
- What was confirming?
- What is now clearer for you?
- What will you now do differently?
- What is the one most important thing you will do next?

LEADERSHIP ATTRIBUTE 7: APPRECIATION

'The deepest principle in human nature is a craving to be appreciated.'
William James

Value others

There is nothing more motivating than to be given a sincere compliment by someone you respect. The importance of recognition and the approval of others is part of the human experience. The leadership behaviours that are grouped in this category and that define appreciation as a motivator are: noticing the strengths of others and telling them what you see, saying thank you when appropriate, and acknowledging and encouraging others as you take an interest in what others do and how they do it.

Being noticed by the principal was mentioned 35 times in the interviews, indicating how important this sub-factor of the attribute of appreciation is to inspirational leadership. As one teacher said, 'When I say he has his finger on the pulse, it might appear I mean the principal is competent, and that is important, but I actually mean he has noticed what I am doing and what I have contributed. My comment is more about how I feel, valued and understood, and less about what he is doing.'

A study found that when people knew they were being watched their performance improved. This is called the 'Hawthorne effect'. It originates from an experiment in the 1920s at Western Electric's Hawthorne Works. Elton Mayo and his colleagues examined how changing conditions such as lighting affect performance. Surprisingly, performance increased not only with better lighting but also when the light was dimmed, suggesting that just watching teams influenced productivity more than the changes in the workplace itself.

Other ways teachers were inspired was by being thanked or praised. Being noticed, thanked or praised makes teachers feel acknowledged and valued, so the relationship between the principal and the staff member is strengthened (Locklear et al., 2020). Teachers in my research agreed and commented that when they felt unappreciated they tended to act out, and as one teacher said, 'I can be naughty.' Much of the staff's complaining, gossiping and blaming can be linked back to feeling insignificant in some way, seeking to be heard or seen (Sinek, 2024). Additionally, the literature review reported the concept of appreciation being highly motivating (Henley, 2022) and included several studies on the importance of building status (Hills, 2014; Keltner, 2017).

Gordon (2022) argues that giving rewards after desirable behaviours is a way of closing off the habit loop. If staff feel rewarded in some way by the chemical cocktail of dopamine and oxytocin, they are more likely to repeat the behaviour that has been rewarded. School staff commented that they would prefer to be rewarded as a group rather than be individually praised. This view aligns with what was found in the literature review (Van Bavel & Packer, 2016). Status was not mentioned in the staff interviews, but school staff clearly expressed that making the team feel valued or significant is an important attribute of a principal's leadership. I would argue that school principals know that this is important, but do not find time in their busy schedules to transform their intentions into actions to the degree they would like to. Additionally, in Australia, it is culturally discouraged to discuss status and put yourself forward to be praised.

The power of praise

There has been much discussion about the ineffectiveness of extrinsic rewards to boost performance and inspire workers across schools, sport and industry. Jim Tressel (2001) is a football coach. He noticed that the performance of his football team had significantly declined over time. He observed that players had been rewarded with a sticker by the previous coach if they had kicked a goal or performed well. When he made changes by rewarding the whole team every time anyone in the team scored a touchdown as a group incentive, almost immediately the team showed improvements, and in addition they won a national championship the following year (Bavel et al., 2018). In the interviews school staff mirrored this belief and shared that they preferred the school to provide team rewards and symbols of success. They expressed that the collective celebration inspired them to engage, collaborate and share stories, which was highly motivating.

A handwritten letter

In his book *The Teacher Who Changed My Life*, Nicholas Gage (1989) was struggling with school studies and challenges at home after his family was torn apart during the Greek Civil War. Eleni, one of his teachers, had noticed his difficulties and gave him a handwritten note telling him she believed in his ability to succeed and encouraging him to rise above his challenges. Gage kept the note for years as a reminder of his teacher's faith in him. He felt the note had been a guiding force in a difficult time and a symbol of strength, reminding him of his potential. In his memoir, Gage explains how this simple handwritten note from a teacher helped shape who he is today, having a lifelong influence and leading him to become a journalist and writer.

When I walk around schools throughout Australia, I often see an old thank you note tacked to the board at a teacher's desk. It is a sign that teachers appreciate such notes of encouragement and that they leave an indelible mark on a person's life long after the author has moved on.

Feeling appreciated and acts of kindness

In a 2013 study, Adam Grant explored how recognising and appreciating employee contributions can significantly boost engagement and performance. The research was conducted in a call centre, where employees were randomly assigned to one of two groups: a 'control group' that received no specific recognition, and an 'appreciation group' that received personalised notes of gratitude from their supervisors. Gratitude is affirming what is good. Experiencing gratitude activates the reward systems in the brain and changes our neural pathways associated with empathy and bonding.

The results showed that employees who were recognised for their contributions displayed a significant increase in motivation, job satisfaction and overall engagement. Grant's study also revealed that employees who felt appreciated were more likely to put extra effort into their work and were more inclined to go beyond their required duties. These employees exhibited stronger feelings of belonging and connection to the organisation, which fostered a sense of commitment and loyalty (Grant, 2013). The findings suggest that even small gestures of appreciation can have a profound impact on employee wellbeing and productivity. Recognition, when genuine and personalised, creates a culture of appreciation that not only improves individual performance but also contributes to the overall success of the organisation.

Dr James Kirby, a clinical psychologist from the University of Queensland, said it is not uncommon to experience a 'feel good rush of endorphins' after you have been kind to someone (2018). He examined over 1000 brain scans and observed that acts of kindness activate the reward centre of the brain (Kirby, 2018). This would suggest that principals also feel good when they provide praise or thank a team member for work well done. On the other hand, gossiping negatively about team members was mentioned several times in the interviews as a behaviour that was found undesirable in inspirational principals. The teachers clearly felt this was a game changer for them in regard to inspiration, as it was expressed across various case studies. An associate professor at the University of Central Florida who is an expert in leadership and management found in a study of 204 employees that gossiping negatively about colleagues was significantly reduced when the leader role-modelled gratitude, such as by writing handwritten thank you notes and building a culture of appreciation and gratitude.

You can draw up your own appreciation plan by using the suggestions shown in Table 21.

Daily	Notice someone doing something right.
Weekly	Write a handwritten thank you note.
Monthly	Highlight a success or strength of a team member in a staff newsletter or meeting.
Annual	Do three random acts of kindness.

Tables 21: Appreciation table

The following phases can help people feel appreciated:

- You are good at that because…
- I will be there.
- I have noticed how you did that.
- I could not have done that without you.

- I trust your judgment.
- I'm proud to know you.
- You always add a polish to everything.
- Keep being you. It matters.
- You bring something unique to the team.
- If it wasn't for you…
- I am grateful that you are…
- I can do better.

Takeaways

- Humans crave appreciation.
- If you make someone feel important, they will come back.
- The act of being noticed and watched is highly motivating.
- Schools that build cultures that reward the behaviour they want to see more of perform better.
- Collective rewards boost team performance.
- Acts of kindness activate the reward centre in the brain and have been associated with high motivation levels.
- Gratitude is affirming what is good and impacts on the reward centre of the brain.

Reflection and journaling

- What ideas emerged?
- What are your insights and learnings?
- What are your challenges?
- What was confirming?
- What is now clearer for you?
- What will you now do differently?
- What is the one most important thing you will do next?

LEADERSHIP ATTRIBUTE 8: COLLABORATION

*'A genuine leader is not a searcher of consensus,
but a moulder of consensus.'*
Martin Luther King Jr

Be a moulder of consensus

Collaboration builds collective efficacy and ownership, and gives us inner knowledge of the hidden rules and engagement levels in teams. An effective leader consults widely and draws out the collective expertise of the team to make sound decisions. The leadership behaviours that are captured in this category and that inspire and engage are: working on a problem together, seeking the views and ideas of others, holding conversations for shared understanding, pooling expertise to problem-solve and innovate, building collective ownership and listening to all the voices as an inclusive practice.

The leadership work is the influence

Jason Simpson, a secondary school head of department, recalls a defining moment that shaped his understanding of influence and leadership:

> *When our principal approached me with a new numeracy initiative, he told me he believed I had the expertise to bring it to life. His confidence in me was energising. I felt honoured and motivated to take the lead. Over the next few weeks, I poured myself into developing a comprehensive plan. When I returned to present it, I was eager to drive it forward. But then he said something that completely shifted my perspective. 'This looks great,' he said. 'I want you to present it at next week's staff meeting, but I also want you to*

understand something: if the staff don't support it, we're not going ahead.' I was taken aback. 'What do you mean?' I asked. He replied, 'This was your idea. If staff aren't on board, there's no point. It needs to be something they choose to support.' I left that conversation feeling slightly deflated. But later it clicked: he wasn't undermining my work. He was teaching me one of the most powerful leadership lessons I've ever learnt. Leadership isn't about imposing ideas on others. It's about inspiring them to take ownership, to believe in the vision themselves. My ability to influence is the leadership work.

That insight transformed my approach. I revisited my plan, made a few strategic tweaks, and carefully crafted my presentation to focus on building collective efficacy. I went into that staff meeting not with the mindset of 'Here's what we're doing to you' but with the intention of saying 'Here's something I believe in; let's explore it together.' The staff embraced the initiative. We implemented it, and it turned out to be a great success. But more importantly, I left that experience with a completely different understanding of influence. True leadership lies in collaboration, in listening, in bringing others through an experience and in growing alongside those you lead. That moment changed everything for me.

Bring people along with you

IBM's research involving over 1600 CEOs in 64 countries concluded that the ability to collaborate with colleagues is one of the top three most important leadership traits (Levin, 2017). Two Australian studies in schools showed that teachers have a preference for collaborative decision-making and welcome opportunities to share their ideas (Avenell, 2015; Cunningham, 2014). A study by Decety et al. (2010) showed that cooperation elicited greater activity in the orbitofrontal cortex than competition, indicative of the reward response. Similarly, Rilling et al. (2002) found elevated activity in the ventral striatum, an area associated with reward processing, when participants observed cooperation. Accordingly, Bavel et al. (2018) inferred that the act of cooperation may bolster 'in group' identification, activating the reward centres of the brain and leading to an increased willingness to cooperate in the future, creating a feedback loop for collaboration.

Working together as the focus

Alan Mullally served as president and chief executive officer of the Ford Motor Company and is known for the way he transformed Ford into one of the world's leading automobile companies. He was named one of the world's 30 best CEOs by *Barron's* and appeared in *Time* magazine's list of the world's most influential people. Under Mulally's leadership, Ford went from losing $12.6 billion in 2006 to achieving record profitability by 2010.

Mullally was renowned for the way he could unite people, his collaborative approach taking centre stage in his success. He nurtured his 'working together leadership and management system', which was the cornerstone of his leadership, and established a deeply connected and collaborative culture.

In brief, the collaborative strategies included: all stakeholders at all levels understanding the vision; weekly meetings where participants reported green (on track), yellow (concerns) and red (serious issues), with the intent of problem-solving together rather than focusing on judgment or blame; a teamwork focus across levels breaking down silos; unifying communication; encouraging a positive improvement focus and fun; accountability in aligning the work to customer needs; and data-driven decision-making.

Insight is the key to collaboration

A key purpose of collaboration is to draw out the collective expertise from the team. To do so requires a setting that is conducive to generating ideas, so that people are more able to experience an 'aha moment'. Studies of the brain have shown that insight requires specific conditions (Jung-Beeman et al., 2008), and recent studies confirm five specific factors:

1. Contribute state – calm and not stressed
2. Trance-like state – self-reflective
3. Not focused directly on the issue or problem
4. Prior thinking about the problem or goal
5. No interruptions – quiet time.

To create a setting for innovation during collaboration, participants need to reduce their cognitive load before a meeting. Arriving on cognitive overload after the school day is not going to be helpful. Either call the meeting in the morning when everyone is fresh after a good night's sleep or have a break before you start or run an activity to destress. Ensure the conversation is not interrupted and participants are not distracted.

Draw out the collective expertise

Teams have diverse backgrounds, experience, egos, personalities, agendas and fears, making teams a minefield of emotion. Collaboration needs to be taught and modelled; it doesn't just happen. Table 22 shows seven ways of working. Working together and sharing isn't enough; rather; the aim is to pool expertise for improved ideas as shown in Stage 7.

Stage		What you see	What you think
1	Combat	Game playing	I will walk over you to get what I want.
2	Compliance	Working in isolation	I will do it because I have to. Just tell me what you want.
3	Competition	Working to win	It is important to be right, win and appear competent all the time.
4	Congeniality	Being nice to each other	It is important to keep everyone happy.
5	Cooperation	Sharing and helping one another	I am willing to share my expertise to help others.
6	Collaboration	Challenging and supporting one another	We are one team and we debate the issue and speak up.
7	Creativity	Drawing out the collective voice to design something new	Let's pool our expertise and build something together that is better than we could do alone.

Table 22: The seven ways of working (Newman, 2010)

Once the team knows what collaboration looks and sounds like, the next step is to practise using steps when collaborating to problem-solve and make decisions. One collaborative process that can be applied to schools is detailed in Table 23.

Step	Phase	Purpose
1	Purpose	Explain the why and purpose.
2	Research	Collect relevant data and examine research.
3	Consultation	Listen to all the voices. Address fears. Show the benefits.
4	Decision-making	Use a SWOT analysis to make the decision not consensus. Look through the ten windows.
5	Planning	Design a plan with actions, strategies, success criteria, roles, resources, training required. Persistence and consistence.
6	Ownership	Remain flexible and adaptable.
7	Implementation	Set up systems to shape the desired behaviour. Adopt an all-in approach.
8	Review	Review and refine.

Table 23: Steps of a collaboration process

Listen to all the voices

Ensure that the loudest, smoothest and most confident talkers are not the only voices that offer solutions and ideas. These are some considerations:

- Use a protocol that requires everyone to share their thoughts and one person speaking at a time.
- Let people know before the meeting what decision needs to be made and how and ask them to come prepared to share an evidence-based perspective.
- Explain why the decision is important.
- Facilitate the conversation so that one person can't dominate and everyone is courteous.
- Encourage and model debate.

- Increase psychological safety by sharing in pairs initially, then form small groups to respond to prepared questions and then report back to the wider group.
- Use a case study showing different perspectives.
- Explain that introverts might need more time to process a new idea, as they process internally, while extroverts draft out loud, but it is what they say at the end that counts.

Takeaways

- Collaboration is about building buy-in so people want to be part of the change process.
- Drawing on the collective expertise of diverse perspectives generates ideas better than one brain can produce.
- Embed protocols to ensure all voices are heard, not just the loud or more confident.
- Insight generation requires five specific conditions.
- When you are experiencing high cognitive load, it is not the best time to be innovative.
- What you build together you won't tear down.

Reflection and journaling

- What ideas emerged?
- What are your insights and learnings?
- What are your challenges?
- What was confirming?
- What is now clearer for you?
- What will you now do differently?
- What is the one most important thing you will do next?

LEADERSHIP ATTRIBUTE 9: COMMUNICATION

*'The words of a leader matter.
They either inspire or incite.'*
President Joe Biden

Be a meaning-maker and agent of change

Masterful communication and leadership go hand in hand. When we are dealing with humans who have different brains, belief systems, passions and fears, in a world where disinformation, misinformation and conspiracy theories are the norm, we need to be able to explain motives and decisions. School principals will be served well if they see their role as meaning-making, being able to communicate why and how a decision was made. The way something is communicated can influence what people hear through their own filters and impact the interpretation of the message. The meaning can be manipulated and misrepresented, so it requires careful delivery, especially as others repeat what they think they have heard you say.

Active listening and candid communication were reported by teachers as the most desirable attributes in a principal's communication. In organisations too large for the principal or CEO to connect with all individuals one on one, communication and trust are the first things to decline. As discussed previously, Professor Dunbar believes that the size of our neocortex correlates with the number of people we can build meaningful relationships with, and as the organisation grows in staff numbers, other leaders need to be established in order to sustain trust and clear communication. The leadership behaviours that are captured in this category are: being able to have candid conversations, seeking and providing feedback, the ability to simplify complex messages, active listening, pass-the-salt tone, meaning-making, compelling speeches and storytelling, tailoring what you say to match the type of relationship (close, personal, new) and clarity of message.

Being a master communicator is a big call. Your voice plays a major role in how you are viewed as a communicator. The components of volume, pitch, speed, inflection and clarity contribute to how we sound to other people, which carries more weight and is more revealing than the words we use (Gordon, 2020). The voice reveals clues about our intent and how we feel. The tone also projects sarcasm, confidence, certainty, disapproval and anxiety. Leaders need to understand that when they speak, people will be listening and will be perceiving much more than just the words, such as hidden agendas.

In their study, Hackman and Johnson (2009) highlighted that communication is not only about conveying information but is also about building relationships, where leaders encourage open dialogue, understand diverse perspectives, motivate their teams and resonate with their messages. Leaders who are excellent communicators are more likely to create a sense of psychological safety, where employees feel valued, heard and empowered to contribute their ideas (Edmondson, 1999). Moreover, the research showed that poor communication often leads to confusion, low morale and decreased productivity. On the eve of his election win on 21 May 2022, Anthony Albanese, the Australian Prime Minister, made a statement that resonated with Australians. He said, 'It says a lot about our great country that a son of a single mum who was a disability pensioner, who grew up in public housing… can stand before you tonight as Australia's Prime Minister.' This statement resonated deeply with Australians from humble or disadvantaged backgrounds. It was a symbol of what is possible and promoted a sense of hope and national pride in fairness and opportunity. He also said that night, 'No one left behind because we should always look after the disadvantaged and the vulnerable but also no one held back, because we should always support aspiration and opportunity.' This inspired compassion and ambition, both of which the Australian community needed to hear at that time.

Clear, calm communication in a crisis

The Apollo 13 mission in 1970 is remembered as a technical triumph but also as an example of leadership through masterful communication. The flight was put at risk when an oxygen tank exploded and damaged its systems, putting the three astronauts onboard in grave danger. Gene Kranz, the flight director, faced an uncertain emergency situation. He was clear, calm and direct in how he communicated with and motivated his team by giving them a common sense of purpose, stating, 'Failure is not an option.' He communicated the urgency of the situation without panic, maintained a steady flow of information, empowered the team through innovation and collaboration, built confidence with motivational language and broke down complex problems into manageable tasks. He communicated the role of everyone in the team based on their skill set.

One of the pivotal moments was the improvisation of a carbon dioxide filter to keep the astronauts alive. Kranz's team had to build a device using only the limited materials available onboard the spacecraft. His calm yet directive communication style empowered engineers to think creatively under pressure. Against all odds, Apollo 13's crew returned to Earth safely. Kranz's leadership and communication skills not only saved lives but also set a benchmark for crisis management. His ability to balance decisiveness with empathy and clarity with inspiration remains a model of communication for leaders in any field.

Open and transparent communication

Men's research (2014) aimed to determine how the communication style and behaviours of leaders influence team performance, motivation and satisfaction. He found that leaders who had open, empathetic, transparent communication were rated significantly higher in leadership effectiveness. Employees who felt informed and listened to by their leaders reported higher job satisfaction and were more engaged in their work. Moreover, transparent communication fostered trust and a sense of inclusion, contributing to a positive organisational culture. The research surveyed 210 employees across industries, asking them to rate their leaders on communication effectiveness including clarity, feedback quality and listening skills. In addition, 15 managers were interviewed to investigate communication approach and style. Listening and providing timely feedback was valued highly by workers.

Prime for conversational chemistry

We can learn much from the applied neuroscience when it comes to how to communicate more effectively. Table 24 shows that the brain chemicals have a role in the impact we have on behaviour and how someone feels.

	Prime	Brain chemical	Behaviour
P	Personalise	Increase oxytocin	Build trust and rapport. Show warmth. Make eye contact. Ask a question rather than tell. Use their name.
R	Reward	Dose of dopamine	Provide a reward cue. Acknowledge and notice a strength. Set a compelling purpose.
I	Identify	Reduce cortisol	Identify the source of anxiety. Ask permissions. Provide choice.
M	Mood	Increase serotonin	Model a calm composure. Use pass-the-salt tone and positive framing. Be non-judgmental.
E	Encourage	Stimulate adrenaline, noradrenaline and acetylcholine	Stimulate and energise to take action with a compelling story or metaphor that provides clarity and interest. Maximise attention.

Table 24: PRIME for conversational chemistry

Frame the message in a strategic way

As I followed school principals around in their day-to-day duties, I noticed that they all used strategic phrases that strengthened their influence. They called upon these phrases to diffuse tension, respond to people's world views and communicate the key message. Some examples are shown in Table 25.

Types	Example
Metaphoric phrases	We need to get our ducks in a line. What are your lower-hanging fruit? Are these rocks, pebbles or sand?
Normalising	What you are saying is called imposter syndrome. Many leaders report feeling like that in your position. That is normal.
Bottom lining	The evidence isn't there to support that grade. (Stating what has been said in less than 15 words to get to the real issue.)
Priming	This event is going to be very exciting.
Paraphrasing	I am hearing you say you are not satisfied with this.
Expectations	At the end of the day, we want to see… Be mindful of the importance of…
Coaching	What makes you say that? What aren't you saying that needs to be said? What is the real issue here?
Storytelling	Something that I saw that worked well was…
Permissions	Are you open to… May I ask you some questions around that? Can we discuss the impact of that?
Positive framing	What have you learnt from that? What could you do next to move that forward? Perhaps she isn't bossy, she might just be very proactive.
Use of pronouns	Use 'we' and 'our' more than 'I' and 'me'.
De-escalating	I could have done better. What am I missing here?

Table 25: Strategic conversational tactics

'When you talk, you are only repeating what you already know. But if you listen, you may learn something new.'

The Dalai Lama

Non-defensive language

Positive framing and encouragement will have more influence than the language of power. Table 26 shows there is power in language.

Power language	Helpful language
No need to be so emotional. You will follow the school's policy on this.	Yes, you make a strong stand. We also need to be mindful that...
This is wrong. You missed the point.	You said... Are you able to tell me how you arrived at that point.
I don't agree. You need to fix the issue.	I have a different perspective on that.
I don't want to do that...	I can see why that would bother you. How can we manage around the issue of...
Sam is silly for doing that.	We need to come back to why we are doing this and that is...
I like working with you but...	We agreed that we would...
I have a problem with the way you did that.	We have a problem here, so let's explore what might have contributed to this and how we might address it.
Fair go, Sam. I think you need to be quiet and allow others to speak.	Thank you for your input, Sam. Now I would like to hear from everyone in the team.
I think there is only one way forward.	Let's hear some different ways we might look at this.
This is too hard. I give up.	Look how far we have come. You have shown stickability. What is your next step?
I have no time.	What can you move or let go of to get this done?
We can't do it. We are up against the best team in the world.	We love a challenge. We only get stronger when the competition is tough.
I have tried three times to give up smoking. I give up.	You have tried to kick a very powerful habit. I admire your strength. You are so close.

Power language	Helpful language
I failed. I will never be able to get there.	Now that you have learnt so much about the goal and yourself, you are in a much better position to nail it.
Why didn't you copy me into your emails?	I trust your judgment on the detail. Just let me know the bigger developments.

Table 26: Power language

Story and metaphors build clarity

As described in *The Leadership Quarterly*, charismatic leaders use storytelling and metaphors to frame challenges in a way that inspires innovation (Antonakis et al., 2011). An article from Johns Hopkins Carey Business School reviewed 50 years of leadership communication research, showing that charismatic leaders effectively use stories and metaphors, convey optimism, and emphasise collective history. These communication strategies significantly influence and inspire followers. Leverage social proof by using testimonials and endorsements, as people are influenced by what others are doing.

Telling stories stimulates the brain's emotive response and engages the reticular activating system (RAS) so people pay attention and are more likely to remember. The RAS pays attention to anything that is funny, unusual, unexpected, new, dangerous, interesting, important or pleasurable (Newman, 2022). A speaker has 30 seconds to grab the attention of the audience (Gordon, 2020). How could you incorporate one or more of the FUUNDIIP factors listed below in your next compelling story to get a key message across?

FUUNDIIP attention-grabbers:

- **F**unny
- **U**nusual
- **U**nexpected
- **N**ew
- **D**angerous
- **I**nteresting
- **I**mportant
- **P**leasurable

On a recent work trip to Canada, I was keynote at the Ulead Conference in Banff. The other keynote speaker was the former first lady of Iceland, Aliza Reid, a professional author and remarkable storyteller. At dinner the night before the conference, Aliza held our attention with compelling stories about her life, and she summed it up nicely in her keynote when she said, 'Stories help us understand the world and they help us navigate future challenges.'

Establishing a common language

Creating a shared common language to bring about unity and understanding is impactful. These terms are a sample of what this could look like, but there is a range of topics that you could apply this to, such as pedagogy and curriculum terms. These terms below can be used with a team when debriefing events:

- **Gorillas:** The things you miss: What didn't we see?
- **Butterflies:** The turning points: Are there any seemingly insignificant events that triggered a significant impact down the track?
- **Elephants:** The things we avoid: What aren't we saying that needs to be said?
- **Alligators:** The distractions: Did anything keep us so busy we didn't get to our main game?
- **Black swans:** The unexpected things: The things that hit you out of nowhere.

Takeaways

- To hold the authority in the room, the leader needs to be calm, clear, concise, relevant and true.
- How we sound has more impact than our words.
- Tone is 50 per cent of the impact.
- Leaders can learn to prime conversational chemistry to improve their communication success.
- A leader benefits from using a toolkit of strategic phrases to improve influence.
- A leader uses positive framing rather than power language.

- A speaker has 30 seconds to hook the attention of the listener, so using the FUUNDIIP factors in a compelling story is influential.
- Schools establish a shared common language to build unity and purpose.
- Storytelling and metaphors are powerful ways to communicate a key message.
- Effective communication requires repetition of the key messages.

Reflection and journaling

- What ideas emerged?
- What are your insights and learnings?
- What are your challenges?
- What was confirming?
- What is now clearer for you?
- What will you now do differently?
- What is the one most important thing you will do next?

LEADERSHIP ATTRIBUTE 10: PURPOSE

'If one does not know to which port one is sailing, no wind is favourable.'
Roman philosopher

Do what matters most

For the growth of the organisation, the team requires a clear sense of purpose. A compelling purpose is very motivating and unifying for a team. The leadership behaviours that are captured in the category of purpose are: explaining the why, forming a philosophical base with underpinning research, visioning a preferred future to work towards, establishing a road map to get there and ensuring everyone is working on the work that matters.

Teachers rated 'explaining the why' at the top of their list for the category of purpose. They were inspired by principals who explained intent and reasons behind actions. Outlining a clear purpose and vision of a preferred future was important to them. A message is stronger if it is repeated over time by several members of the leadership team. It needs to be heard several times to allow it to be encoded in the brain over time to consolidate long-term memory. What is in the leader's head is not always what is clear in the team's head.

All state schools in Queensland are expected to develop a three-year strategic plan for the management of their school, outlining a road map for their improvement agenda. I have not worked with a school as yet across states and systems that did not have a vision statement for their school. School leaders need a clear sense of direction, to know where they are going and why (Kouzes & Posner, 1990). Teachers expressed this view by stating in the interviews that they would like a strategic plan, so they knew where they were on the road map.

Understand the core values and true purpose

In 2006, Albert Park Secondary College (APC), a public secondary school, closed after a loss of confidence caused enrolments to plummet to 200. The old buildings were bulldozed and a new school was designed and built from the ground up, under the extraordinary leadership of Steven Cook. In 2021, APC was voted Australian School of the Year. I have had the pleasure of working with Steven and his staff, and there is much that sets APC apart, but what stood out was Steven's clear vision and purpose for his school.

Every staff member I met with was able to talk about the school purpose and values with a great deal of pride and consistent detail, and more importantly, I could see those values lived out in their practice and conversations. They knew why they were doing the work and how far they had come towards their goals. As Steven wrote in his book, 'there is no point bothering to formulate a vision for a great school if it never makes it off the page.' It is clear that he has reflected deeply and often on what education really means. He believes a principal's role is to be the 'defender of the concept of education. In other works, be a moral leader'. That belief pulses through the culture of APC, where moral purpose and core values guide everything. They ensure that the students sit at the centre of everything they do.

I asked Steven how he managed to establish full engagement in a shared vision. He stated that he loathes what he calls volunteerism: 'The slow drip of creative death.' He expects a 'no opt out, all in' approach to ensure high standards. 'When we make a decision to move in a new direction, it is a commitment for everyone.' Imagine if a bank or hospital said, 'I don't like this new way of doing things. I think I will stick to my old ways because it feels more comfortable.' What would happen? 'Don't allow volunteerism to determine what happens in your school,' he recommended. He could not have put it more eloquently.

Importantly, this approach does not stifle creativity or autonomy. In fact, APC actively seeks out unique teacher expertise and celebrates it. They have a dedicated recruiting panel that has clear and consistent criteria for hiring. They seek people who are active in their field – artists, musicians, poets and scientists – people who have a demonstrated passion and capacity in their chosen profession. They also have something up their sleeve that is somewhat quirky. They seek colleagues who have done something interesting or special with their life. For example, they have a maths teacher who travelled the world and photographed Grand Prix races. This intentional focus on expertise and attitude protects the school from mediocrity and resistance, which can derail progress. As Steven puts it, 'A principal's role is to ensure that every child has access to the best teacher, which means that it is all in.' This is only possible when teachers are willing to collaborate, share best practice, and commit to continual learning and growth. I witnessed this culture in action: teachers leading workshops for their peers with confidence and professionalism. Expertise is not hidden at APC; it's elevated and shared.

Steven believes that 'the best way to start developing coherence and community of purpose in a school is to hone your values into simple messages and state them regularly. When you are sick of talking about your values, most of your teachers, staff and students are probably just hearing them for the first time.' At APC, those values are heard, seen and felt, every single day.

A clear vision

The relationship between leadership and purpose has been well documented. Bavel et al. (2018) argue that leadership is fundamentally about creating a feeling of common purpose – known as a social identify. A 1989 study by Korn-Ferry International affirms that being able to articulate a vision and strategic direction is an important competency. Later, in the year 2000, they conducted another study involving 1500 executives in 20 countries and found that the leadership trait most frequently described was the ability to convey a strong sense of vision. In their most recent study, 75 per cent said that purpose and vision are essential today. Clearly, articulating a vision and being forward-thinking is a long-standing competency expected in leadership. The team needs to understand the strategic direction of their leaders. The ability to explain what success looks like in a compelling way – what you are trying to achieve, why it is the right direction, why it will be better, what the results look like – is essential to the motivational levels of a team. If staff don't understand the purpose, they will not believe in what they are doing and their motivation levels will decline (Day, 2015; Sinek, 2024; Willink & Babin, 2017).

Identify your purpose

Work out your purpose guided by the ancient Japanese ikigai illustrated in Figure 10. Asking yourself four questions around what you should be doing to meet your needs can be very satisfying.

Ikigai questions:

- What do you love?
- What are you good at?
- What does the world need?
- What are people willing to pay for?

Figure 10: Ikigai model

Be a strategic leader not an accidental manager

Once you have identified your true purpose, understanding the difference between the operational work and the strategic work is easier, as they are both part of inspirational leadership. If your team knows the difference, they are more likely to invest in the improvement work rather than always being seduced by the easier management work. There is an old tale told in leadership that starts with 'Babies are floating down the river and many of them are drowning. What would you do?' Of course, you would dive in and save them. This is reactive and has a short-term impact; however, they are still floating down the river, keeping you busy. What you need to do is be proactive, step back, delegate and head upriver to find the old man throwing them in and address the root cause. If you are always doing the operational management work, you will have a tidy department or organisation but you will always be reactive. Influential leadership requires investment in the proactive strategic leadership work.

This type of work involves the human element of building capacity, changing thinking, visioning, setting standards and shifting workplace cultures. It is much more difficult. In fact, you can spend the whole day operating in the strategic leadership space and have nothing to show for it at the end of the day, because it involves conversing with people. They say, 'You lead the people stuff and manage everything else.' There is no right balance; it all depends on how long you have been in the job and what your role is.

Table 27 shows the nature of the work in both categories.

Strategic leadership work	Operational management work
Shift cultures	Policy and systems
Change behaviours	Clarity of roles
Raise standards	Accountability and goals
Coach people	Mentoring and feedback
Set tone	Resourcing
Collaborate and unite	Induction and training
Extract expertise and ideas	Teaching, curriculum
Influence thinking	Finance and facilities
Inspire and motivate	Planning
Change leadership	Checklists and to-do lists
Create conditions for others to lead	Timetabling
Line of sight	Events

Table 27: Strategic and operational work

*'You can't lead by personality alone.
You have to be more strategic than that.'*
Judi Newman

Do you have balance?

It is easy for the nature of your work to tilt towards your comfort zone and personality, but an influential leader has a balance of whoness, whatness, whyness and howness. A summary is shown in Table 28.

WHYNESS	WHATNESS	WHONESS	HOWNESS
Purpose	Results	Character	Execution
Direction	Competence	Warmth	Planning
Vision	Structures	Humility	Steps
Values	Systems	Integrity	Research
Meaning	Policy	Rapport	Momentum
Priorities	Tasks	Trust	Culture
Beliefs	Strategy	Tone	Change
Precision	KPIs	Strength	Learning
Clarity	Accountability	Inspiration	Training
Line of sight	To-do lists	Tough-mindedness	Protocols
Big picture	Role clarity	Positivity	Innovation
Mission	Goals	Relationships	Process

Table 28: Whyness, whatness, whoness and howness (Newman, 2022)

There are four aspects of leadership that are vital to building effective teams that play at their best. These are:

1. **The 'what':** This is about getting the task done to get results. Leaders need to get results. They need to be seen as competent.
2. **The 'why':** This is about having clarity of purpose. Leaders need to be able to communicate a vision so clearly that others see where they are going and why.
3. **The 'who':** This is about being able to build trust and therefore influence others. It is about character strength.
4. **The 'how':** This is about process. The process of how we get there and execute can be just as important as the outcome.

We need to start with the **why** because it gives us purpose and therefore directs where our energy goes. It also is the anchor for our decision-making that keeps us on the direct path to the results we want. However, having said that, it is the **who** that will make all the difference. People will work well together if they feel valued and appreciated by each other and the boss. Getting the right people in your team with the right mindset and skillset is the key to success.

So, a leader needs a balance of all four areas of **who**, **what**, **how** and **why** because one is just as important as the others. Failing to incorporate any one of these four components will lead to serious negative consequences for organisational and team performance.

- **who + what + how** (missing the why) = lower performance because people will be off task doing the busy work rather than the work that matters.
- **what + why + how** (missing the who) = a lack of warmth and trust because we need a connection to harness the relationship, and if there is no relationship there is limited information about who you are and what you represent.
- **why + who + how** (missing the what) = slow change because you haven't put the systems and structures in place to shape behaviour and therefore establish a learning and performance culture for results.
- **why + who + what** (missing the how) = lack of ability to easily see how to get from A to B.
- **why + who + what + how balance** = sweet spot. This is where the four components of what, who, why and how overlap and create the 'sweet' spot. This is where a leader aims to be. At this spot, people will have clarity around their role; will know where they are going and why; will know what results are expected; and will feel genuinely appreciated and therefore more likely to be motivated to fully engage.

> *'The future is not some place we are going, but one we are creating. The paths are not to be found but made. And the activity of making them changes both the maker and the destination.'*
>
> John Schaar

Takeaways

- A vision is a preferred future.
- If you can't articulate your vision to others, they will tell you what it is.
- Teams like to have a road map on how to get where they are going.
- Key messages need to be repeated to the whole school community.
- A leader needs to be able to explain what success looks like and be able to take others down the road they would not always go down.
- A leader needs a balance of whyness, whatness, howness and whoness.
- Understand the difference between the strategic leadership work and the operational management work.
- Make room for the strategic leadership work or improvement will be slow.

Reflection and journaling

- What ideas emerged?
- What are your insights and learnings?
- What are your challenges?
- What was confirming?
- What is now clearer for you?
- What will you now do differently?
- What is the one most important thing you will do next?

LEADERSHIP ATTRIBUTE 11: CHALLENGE

*'A leader is a leader who can build other leaders
who can build other leaders.'*
Phil Rylie

Coach the human not the content

Humans need some degree of challenge to be motivated. Too little and they may be bored; too much and they may be stressed. Invest in building capacity in your team to inspire strategic leaders rather than accidental managers. Multiply and amplify your influence by growing other leaders around you. Focus on coaching the human not just the content.

The leadership behaviours that are captured in the category of challenge are: using coaching questions, providing opportunities for growth, offering training and professional development such as professional papers and professional libraries, modelling lifelong learning, providing sound advice and mentorship, keeping others accountable to the priority work, encouraging individuals to step out of their comfort zones, and sharing your self-talk or 'talk outlouds'. Teachers prize coaching questions as a way of inspiring them to build their performance.

Managing, mentoring and coaching

Differentiating your leadership approach to manage, mentor and coach is a useful style for building the performance of others. Managing is about setting up policies and systems for the good order of the school. It usually involves advising. Mentoring is about showing, sharing, demonstrating, shadowing and providing exemplars to support growth and build expertise. Coaching is about asking questions to tap into the potential of the coachee to draw out independent thinking and ownership. It is important to know when to use which approach. Not all situations are appropriate for coaching. A coachee requires some experience. Table 29 below shows that when we are supporting a new person they will require management in the form of an induction program and mentorship first. To build the capacity of an experienced teacher or principal, coaching can be used to extend their capability.

Level	Manage	Mentor	Coach
Dysfunctional	Always	Sometimes	Never
Learning	Often	Often	Rarely
Developing	Often	Often	Sometimes
Functional	Sometimes	Often	Often
Effective	Sometimes	Often	Often
Masterful	Rarely	Sometimes	Often

Table 29: When is the approach appropriate?

Seek and give feedback

Few of us enjoy giving and seeking critical feedback, but it is an excellent way to improve quickly and to build the capacity of other leaders around you. People tend to move away from threat, so the first step is to build feedback into the culture of the workplace so that it is expected and frequent, rather than having one 'big' conversation on a rare occasion. Challenge the assumption that critical feedback makes a person mean. When you say, 'Joan, I noticed that you are late for meetings and often miss deadlines', all Joan hears is, 'Joan, I don't like you.' However, without feedback we never really see ourselves as others see us, because we use filters for self-preservation. Make it clear that feedback is a gift. A helpful question to ask is 'When you get feedback do you get defensive or do you see it as an opportunity to learn?' Focus on the purpose of feedback, which is to help people build and polish their expertise. If the communication is not honest, there will be confusion and many elephants in the room. If there is a particular tricky issue to be discussed, think of the worst that could happen and then start with that: 'John, I want to give you some feedback, but I don't want you to think that you are not considered future management potential. In fact, I want to support your pathway there by coaching you through the minefield.' Ask permission so the person is prepared: 'May I give you some feedback on that?'

See potential

When describing her principal, one teacher said to me, 'He was really great at saying to people: you would be great at that. Why don't you have a go? He was very good at seeing the opportunities for people. Even if they didn't see it themselves, or didn't believe it themselves, he had a really nice way of making that happen for people so they could see their own potential.' This was very motivating.

Serving life up on a silver platter

I remember listening to a story on the radio many years ago. It was about a country in the Middle East that was wealthy in oil. They had contracted a consultant to help them make their people happier. The consultant started with ranking them on the World Happiness Scale (WHS), and they achieved a reasonable score. Over the next few years, the country's officials worked hard at installing a range of services and processes that they believed would make the people happier. They gave every newly married couple a house and land package. They asked the same consultant to return three years later, expecting that they would now proudly see the benefits of all their hard work. Alas, the WHS score had actually dipped significantly. They had taken the challenge out of living by giving everything to people on a silver platter. The previous level of challenge had provided some sense of satisfaction for the citizens, as challenge is motivating. When things come too easily, we can lose our motivation.

Learning conversations

Having a suite of learning conversations in the toolkit is helpful to a leader. Some examples are outlined below. They include a framework for a:

- Coaching conversation
- Mentoring conversation
- Feedback conversation
- Adult conversation
- Conflict-management conversation

- Event-debriefing conversation
- Investigative conversation
- Post-observational brief.

Coaching questions

Leaders ask subjective questions rather than making objective statements. They are curious. Coach the human, not just the content.

In a formal coaching session:

- What do you want to achieve?
- What would success look like to you?
- If you nailed it, what would be different?
- How can I help you with your thinking on that?
- What have you done already?
- What roadblocks do you expect?
- What is this really about?
- What questions does that raise for you?
- What is emerging here for you?
- What are some ways you could tackle this?
- What else?
- What would you like to see happen?
- What would it take to make that happen?
- Which of these ideas are you prepared to action?
- Who or what can help you with that?
- What is the next level of thinking on this?
- What is your next step?
- What is your sureness of success?
- What connections have you made in your thinking?
- What is your new thinking on this?
- What are you now clearer about?

Giving feedback

What do you want me to:

- Start doing?
- Keep doing?
- Stop doing?

Be mindful:

- All feedback has merit, but not all feedback is equal.
- Is the feedback constructive criticism or reflective of their projected fears and ego?
- Do I defend my ground or do I see feedback as an opportunity to learn?
- Ask yourself: 'If 10 per cent of the feedback was true, what would that mean for me?'

The adult conversation

Difficult conversations are the business of an influential leader. If you ignore dysfunctional and serial unhelpful behaviour, your good people will leave. If you don't discuss expectations prior to things going sideways, then you have nothing to anchor into and things will be more stressful when you try to sort it out. Use the steps in the following model to plan the conversation, keeping your part of the conversation clear, concise, relevant and true. This model is called the 'dead fish' conversation because if you don't address chronic unhelpful or dysfunctional behaviour the smell will get worse. The aim is to intervene early and informally at first. If nothing changes, then the situation may require a more formal interaction. Calling it a hard conversation may amplify your anxiety around the expectation of a difficult response. It is really just an adult conversation. Keep your tone 'pass the salt' and respectful and aim to keep the relationship intact. If you are not having the adult conversations, others will notice. Table 30 outlines a helpful framework for an adult conversation. It is modified and informed by Susan Scott's fabulous book *Fierce Conversations* (2010).

Step	Reason
State	State what you want to say in less than 15 words.
Evidence	Provide an example.
Impact	Explain the consequences of the behaviour continuing.
Anchor	Anchor into a place of certainty (role, rule, value, purpose).
Expectation	What needs to happen...?

Step	Reason
Intent	My intent is to work with you to resolve this.
Listen	What is your take on this?
Support	Who can help you with this?

Table 30: The 'dead fish' conversation

Conflict resolution

1. **Permissions:** Do you agree to using the process and being guided by a coach?
2. **Expectations:** What is your goal today? What do you need most from this situation? What do you see as a successful resolution?
3. **Situation:** Tell me what is going on for you. What happened? What do you think other parties would say happened?
4. **Options:** What will work for you in this situation? What other ideas do you need to consider? What might you have to let go of to achieve that? How will you know when you have resolved the conflict? Who or what might help you with that?
5. **Learning:** What are your triggers that you need to prepare for? What might you want to now say differently? What are some challenges you might face? What have you learnt in this situation? What else?

Event debriefing conversations

1. What were we trying to do?
2. What happened?
3. What caused our results?
4. Are we making any assumptions?
5. Where did we hit our objectives?
6. Pinpoint any elephants, butterflies, alligators, swans or gorillas.
7. What can we learn from this?
8. What would we do differently next time?
9. What should we start, keep or stop doing?
10. What now?

Investigative conversation

1. State purpose, roles and process. Provide terms of reference.
2. Tell me what happened? (open question)
3. Tell me more about the part when... (point-in-time question)
4. What were you thinking at that time? (specific question)
5. How did you hurt your foot? (specific question)
6. Who was there? (specific question)
7. Tell me what happened then? (open question)

Post-observation debrief

1. How did that go for you?
2. What worked well?
3. What would you do differently next time?
4. I noticed... (evidence)
5. I noticed... (evidence)
6. I noticed... (evidence)
7. What questions does this raise for you?
8. What support/training would be helpful?
9. What is your key takeaway from this conversation?
10. What is your next step?

Takeaways

- Challenge is motivating until it becomes stress.
- Find the sweet spot between high expectations and support.
- Differentiate your leadership's style to manage, mentor and coach to build the capacity of others through gradual release of responsibility.
- Feedback is a gift and is the best error-detection technique to speed up growth.
- Carry a toolkit of learning conversations so you are not shooting from the hip.
- Leaders see feedback as an opportunity to learn rather than get defensive.
- If you don't have the adult conversations, your good people will leave.

Reflection and journaling

- What ideas emerged?
- What are your insights and learnings?
- What are your challenges?
- What was confirming?
- What is now clearer for you?
- What will you now do differently?
- What is the one most important thing you will do next?

LEADERSHIP ATTRIBUTE 12: AUTONOMY

*'Control leads to compliance,
autonomy leads to engagement.'*
Daniel Pink

Allow some choice within terms of reference

When motivating a team, autonomy builds a sense of control and freedom to choose. Choice is a dominant theme in motivation theory suggesting humans prefer a strong sense of autonomy at work. Choice maintains people's comfort levels. People who believe that they have very little autonomy at work have been found to have heightened levels of cortisol. People understand that high-performance teams have some non-negotiable practices that need to be seen throughout the organisation. However, team members also need some sense of autonomy in how they go about their role.

When we have the opportunity to choose (such as choosing our own food or movie), we experience greater rewards – choice and reward have become so strong in our minds that choice itself is rewarding. A sense of autonomy provides a dopamine hit in the reward centres of our brain. There is much debate about mandating optional professional development and training in a sheep-dip approach. Instead, it might be smarter to make professional development and training so compelling that people want to be part of it. People don't like to be told what to do, so making training a choice can be more effective, as the people who participate will be more fully engaged and willing to take part actively. However, some professional development training is essential and required, so it does need to be mandated. Either way, one of the strongest motivators in the workforce is when everybody is doing it. The challenge is getting people to own their own decision to take part without feeling they have been coerced.

No leader has the 'cognitive capacity, the physical presence or the knowledge of everything' to micromanage every team member (Willink & Babin, 2017, p. 172). They must build the leadership capacity within smaller teams and share their leadership to allow other leaders to make their own decisions, within some non-negotiables and standard operating procedures or parameters. This allows the school principal to be available and free of the detail to see the bigger picture, detect mistakes and assess the outcomes of the team. Conversely, Willink and Babin (2017) point out that the leader needs to be careful not to be too far removed from the coalface; otherwise, they risk becoming disconnected and redundant. They recommend that the leader allow teams to plan the details after being clear about the goal. This way, the team have pooled their expertise and own the process, and the leader can then offer expertise to tighten up the tasks. This type of approach works in schools; it is more likely to grow people and build collective efficacy, as they are all involved in the decision-making. One thing that was very obvious in the school interviews I conducted was that teachers did not like being micromanaged.

Teachers like some sense of autonomy

Tom Melohn, president of North American Tool and Die (NATD), was reported by Kouzes and Posner (1990) as having brought the company into significant profit. When examining his approach to find the answer to his success, they found he inspired people by entrusting skilled team members with the autonomy to do their job. With the increased freedom, work performance increased and the expertise of the team members also improved.

Match autonomy with expertise

When I was seconded to the public service for nearly five years to support the work of school principals, the regional director said to me on my first day, 'If you do nothing else, Judi, I want principals to understand their influence and to see themselves as leaders.' This statement gave me a compelling purpose and showed me immediately that I wasn't going to be micromanaged. He didn't tell me how to do my job but allowed me the freedom to apply my expertise and shape the role into something new that aligned with his vision. He said I could report directly to him and didn't have to clock in and out, freeing me from the constraints of multiple approval layers and public service paperwork. It is much more powerful for people to have clarity around the why of their roles than to be told what to do. Encouragement is often more influential than mandates, especially if the person has a proven success rate and high motivation. This freedom gifted to me built trust both ways. I didn't want to let him down.

Expand choice with tasks

Offer as much choice within a task as possible without weakening the quality of the results or reducing the integrity of the role. For example, if a school has decided to offer lunchtime activities for the students, don't mandate the topics; rather, ask staff what they are interested in and allow them autonomy in how they run their interest area.

Takeaways

- Some sense of autonomy and choice is a strong motivator for performance.
- You can't have autonomy without some non-negotiables and terms of reference.
- If everyone chose their own adventure, there might not be alignment with the strategic vision.
- Communicate the purpose and the why of the training and make it compelling rather than mandate everything.
- One of the most motivating triggers is: everyone wants to do it and everyone is seen to be doing it.
- People don't like to be micromanaged.
- A leader is not micromanaging when they are checking accountability from time to time. You can't raise standards if you don't check and observe.

Reflection and journaling

- What ideas emerged?
- What are your insights and learnings?
- What are your challenges?
- What was confirming?
- What is now clearer for you?
- What will you now do differently?
- What is the one most important thing you will do next?

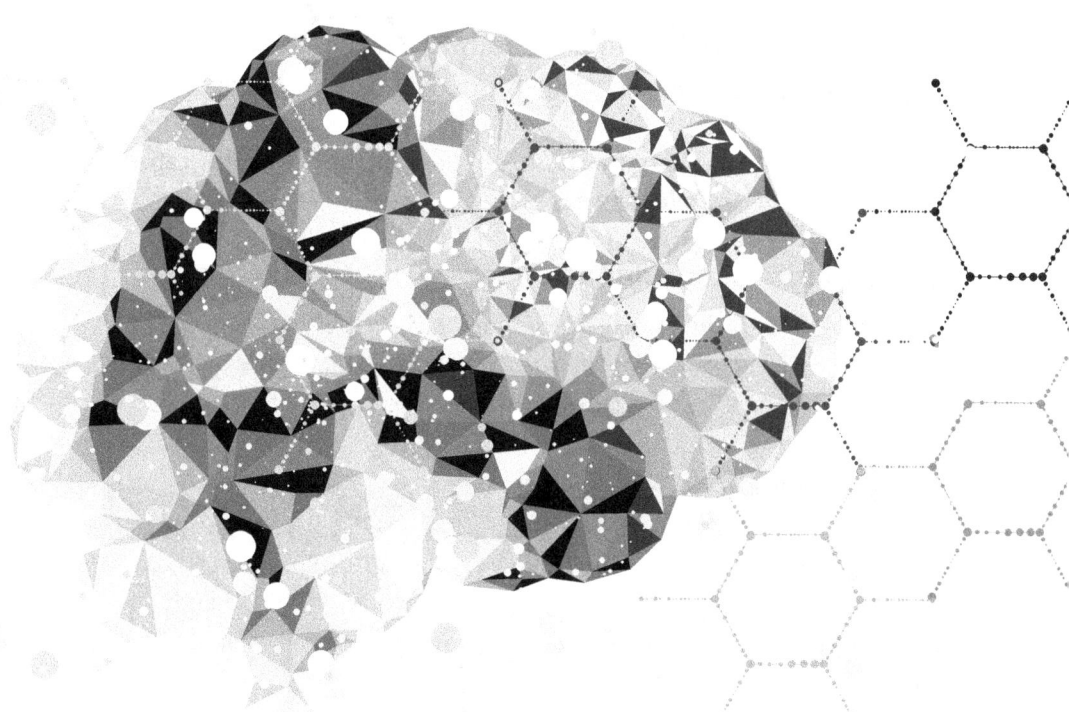

Part 3
Influence Strategies

'Leadership influence is but a moment where you make a positive difference that has lifelong impacts for changed behaviour.'

DR JUDI NEWMAN

A school leader can't lead by personality alone, because they need to be much more strategic about how they drive change. It is therefore helpful to look at influence theory and practical strategies that can be used to boost impact. I have summarised the tools in Table 31 and unpacked each of them in the following pages.

Leadership is about influence

> *'Leadership is the art of getting someone else to do something you want done because he wants to do it.'*
>
> Dwight Eisenhower

	Strategy	Goal
I	Interpersonals	Understand how you turn up. Do you project your intent and strengths or your fears and ego?
N	Needs	Understand your people's needs and align the goals with the ten motivational needs.
F	Fortitude and boundaries	Embed structures that shape desired behaviours, because you can only control your own behaviour.
L	Leadership strength	Understand how to define leadership and what it means to step up your leadership. Know what you should be doing.
U	Understanding bias	Mitigate cognitive bias to strengthen your influence.
E	Emotion	Logic and reason are not always enough to change behaviour. You need to experience an emotion to become part of the change.
N	Neuroplasticity	There is limited behaviour change and learning without neuroplastic changes in the brain over time.
T	Traditions and culture	Start with the leaders first to create a culture that aligns with the purpose and values.
I	Intentional conversations	Be calm, clear, concise, relevant and true to hold the authority in the room.
A	Accountability	Set clear expectations of role and results. If everyone is doing it, it is motivating: all in.
L	Likeability	People like like-minded people who like them.

Table 31: Influential framework

I IS FOR INTERPERSONALS

> *'If you can't be a good role model then you'll just have to be a horrible warning.'*
> Catherine Aird

What we look like and how we sound will be noticed by others and remembered more than what we say (Goman, 2011; Gordon, 2020). So, intent is not enough – you can't see intent. Understanding how we turn up, how we are perceived by others, and knowing our impact on others is essential for leadership influence. Ask someone, 'What is it like to spend five minutes with me?' What would they say? What do people say about you when you leave the room? Do you pause to have a two-way conversation or is it a continuous one-way stream of all the thoughts in your head? Others will see your facial expressions and posture and think they know what you are thinking. Often our brain state drives our posture, reveals itself in the tone of voice we use, and triggers our facial expressions, and the impression others receive may be miles from our intention. In particular, when we are under stress, our body language can project our fears and ego rather than our strengths and intent. The TWICE model captures five useful tips to help us turn up in a way that boosts our influence.

Think twice before you turn up

The first tip is to be mindful of the tone you use. Humans pick up on tone very quickly and make inferences from the clues it presents. Evian Gordon (2020) states that tone has up to 50 per cent impact. Using a teacher or parent tone (where the other person feels they are in trouble or being lectured) is not going to be the best way to influence others. Check your tone and practise using a 'pass the salt' tone, meaning speak in a calm considered way as you would do when asking someone to pass the salt at the dinner table – polite, calm and confident.

Second, warmth is essential. I was running a workshop for around 200 teachers one day, and we were discussing the importance of showing warmth to build rapport. One teacher said, 'I am always friendly and warm.' I had only been there for a day, but I can tell you that she may have been inwardly warm, but to the outside world she appeared sour and tired. To project warmth, others have to feel the warmth, like a cosy fire. You can't control how others feel, but you can control what you do and say to project that warmth. Smiling, encouraging, enquiring and attending to our facial expression is a good starting point for warm interactions.

Third, our interpersonals speak volumes. 'Interpersonals' refers to our facial expression and our posture. Our posture can give away how we are feeling but also can be an indication that we are cold or tired. 'In the future, leaders who still believe that what they say carries more weight than how they look and sound when speaking, will be left wondering why their colleagues don't respect or trust them. Successful leaders will be those displaying body language that is authentically aligned with their verbal messages' (Goman 2011).

Professor Amy Cuddy and her colleagues from Harvard University have shed light on how posture can affect perception. They have studied the way confident people hold themselves and found a correlation between open posture and confidence, and closed posture and lack of confidence. If we make ourselves bigger and more open, such as by raising our arms in the air when we win a race, the posturing triggers a release of dopamine and other brain chemicals that are responsible for the feeling of joy and agency. When we close our body language and act smaller, the opposite occurs. So, next time you are feeling a little chilly, don't wrap your arms around yourself – go and put on a jumper!

Fourth, building credibility through how you communicate can make a big difference to how you are perceived by others. According to the cooperative maximum, a speaker holds more authority in the room if they are clear, concise, relevant and true. Add composure and you have a good recipe for communication. No one likes a leader who waffles.

Finally, do you invest energy and enthusiasm in your response when someone greets you or when you check in with others. Are you mindful about what you say that is responsive to their needs? The conversation is the relationship (Scott, 2010). The TWICE framework, represented in Table 32, captures five key questions about how we turn up.

T	Tone	Do you use 'pass the salt' tone?
W	Warmth	Do you smile, inquire and encourage?
I	Interpersonals	Does your body language match your intent and strengths, or does it project your fears and ego?
C	Credibility	Are you calm, clear, concise, relevant and true?
E	Energy	Do you practise an active contribute response?

Table 32: The TWICE model

The boy with the hat

Once I was working with a group of assistant principals who were just beginning their journey and had signed up for an aspiring leadership program. Before I started, a principal asked me if I could speak to him in private. He said he wanted to apologise for the fact that his assistant principal, Tom (not his real name), would be wearing a cap indoors. He said he had tried to talk Tom into taking off his cap as a mark of respect, but for some reason Tom could not be influenced. He hung onto the habit of wearing a cap backwards, indoors and outdoors, as a part of his sense of identity. The principal said he was certain it didn't have anything to do with his health, as Tom had indicated that it was his right to wear a hat, and 16 earrings in his nose, if he so wished. He made it fairly clear that it was a rebellious message he wanted to project. Over the course of many days together, I could see that Tom was bright and had significant potential for senior leadership. In fact, in many ways he was a shining light. As trust became established in the group over time, we had some very interesting candid conversations about what it meant to lead, what influence looked like, and about personal and professional growth. I felt that Tom knew I had his best interests at heart. I also knew he was committed to making a go of his role and worked very hard. I wasn't interested in changing Tom, as that was up to him, but I was interested in helping him meet his aspirations. Out of the hearing of others, I said to Tom, 'How invested are you in being principal one day, Tom?' He responded, '100 per cent. I love my job and I hope one day I can lead my own school. I have so many ideas and I like working with people.' I asked him, 'Can I give you some feedback in regard to getting there?' Tom replied, 'Please speak freely. I would value your opinion – warts and all.' I dived in, taking him at his word, and said, 'I want others to see your significant potential like I do. You have the skill set to be a principal. However, what people see and talk about is the boy with the hat. They can't see past the hat, Tom. They stop there, so they don't see your strengths.' Tom blinked and stared. He nodded in silence and walked off, processing what I said. The next day, Tom arrived without his hat. He had a pressed linen shirt and looked like a future principal.

We might debate that a hat has nothing to do with our ability to do the job. In many ways, it is of course irrelevant. However, leadership is about influence, and that hat was preventing Tom from influencing in the way he wanted to. He was getting in the way of himself. Despite his strong skill set and kind nature, he lost job opportunities because of the hat, but no one told him because it wasn't politically correct. Whether we like it or not, people judge us by what we look like and how we sound, not just by our words and intent. (Perhaps, I should say a brain judges us that way.) Do you wear any hats in your leadership behaviours?

Reflective questions

- What would someone say if you asked them what it feels like to spend five minutes with you?
- What was a surprise to you, and did your expectation meet their reality?
- In your last speech to staff, would you rate yourself as calm, clear, concise, relevant and true?
- Does your body language match your intent or strengths? How do you know?
- How did you provide an active contribute response to the first five staff you checked in with today?
- On a scale of 1–10 (1 being cold and 10 being very warm) how would people rate your warmth? If your score is low, what can you do to warm up?
- Do you wear any hats in your leadership behaviours?
- Do you smile, encourage and enquire when you have a conversation or do you only give advice?

N IS FOR NEEDS

'Successful relationships require that all parties view getting their core needs met as being legitimate.'
Susan Scott

My own leadership approach changed dramatically when I changed my own mindset from 'I have a team of people who work for me' to 'I work for my team.' This subtle switch meant that as I interacted with an individual, I was thinking about how I could meet their needs. 'What can I say right now to support or grow them? Do they need clarity, autonomy, approval, loyalty, challenge, resources, praise, meaning or a good listener?' Leadership taps into the inner motivations of people.

Maslow's hierarchy was well documented over the decades and his important work is still valid today. A more recent literature review has revealed ten human needs framed in the ESCAPE model (Newman, 2022). It is no surprise that Maslow's needs are inherent in this model. We now understand that there are three needs that are required for survival and seven additional needs.

Humans need some essentials to survive, such as water, food, sleep, sunshine and air, and this can be expanded to include anything that makes us comfortable and keeps us pain-free. Secondly, we need to feel safe, not just physically but psychologically. Individuals have no need or responsibility to share their innermost mental challenges with colleagues, so you may not know what fears and anxieties they are dealing with. The third survival need is connectedness. We now know that having a strong sense of belonging to a social group is not just desirable but essential to our wellbeing. These are the first three human motivational needs for survival.

The next seven motivational needs are in no particular order but will be prioritised differently by different individuals. These are a need for control, challenge, appreciation, pleasure, purpose, exactitude and expectation. The ten needs are outlined in Table 33.

E	Essential	A need for the basic survival comforts: essential physiological needs, such as addressing thirst, hunger, pain, fresh air, sunshine, exercise and sleep.
S	Safety	A need for physical and psychological safety is essential for building trust. This incorporates being mindful of fears, phobias and anxieties.
C	Connectedness	A need for warmth, rapport and unity.
C	Control	A need for choice and freedom.
C	Challenge	A need for achievement, growth and self-actualisation.
A	Appreciation	A need for status, self-esteem and feeling valued.
P	Pleasure	A need for the things we enjoy.
P	Purpose	A need for meaning and a reason.
E	Exactitude	A need for correctness. This is about fairness, truth, justice, ethics and honour.
E	Expectation	A need for certainty, consistency and clarity.

Table 33: The ESCAPE model of motivational needs

Let's explore each of the ten human needs and see why they may be related to motivational levels.

1. **Essential:** Comfort levels will add to your ability to do the job. If you have a toothache or are hungry, you are going to be distracted. Ensure the team has all the basic necessities to keep them comfortable, such as a comfortable chair, a photocopier that is maintained, or flexibility when family crisis calls. It is helpful to take stock of the environment to assess if it meets the essential needs. Does the kitchenette have a microwave? Has everyone access to parking within walking distance? I once had a job where I often had

to park ten blocks away, and if it was raining or 38 degrees, I would feel melted before I started work. I asked about parking and was told there was not enough. First in, first served. Too bad, so sad.

2. **Safety:** This is about creating a workplace culture where you feel comfortable to give feedback, make errors as you learn, question and pose ideas, without judgment, even when there is disagreement. You are not going to approach someone with positional power if it is going to be a career-limiting conversation. If there is low trust in the system and the people around them, people will hold back.

3. **Connectedness:** Team members need to feel like an important part of the tribe and that their role and contribution matter. You can't build trust if you don't have that emotional connection with people (Cuddy, 2022).

4. **Control:** Most teachers understand that schools benefit from some shared non-negotiables. Assuming those essential common practices are in place, teachers reported that they like some sense of autonomy in how they approach the teaching and learning.

5. **Challenge:** Humans are motivated by a sense of challenge and become bored if things are too easy. Personalising the opportunities for every individual to build their expertise will increase work satisfaction.

6. **Appreciation:** Humans have a craving to be appreciated. If you make someone feel important, they will come back. Be mindful that not everyone wants to be thanked or acknowledged in the same way.

7. **Pleasure:** If people enjoy their work, they will be less stressed and perform better. Encourage others to find the joy and laughter in their day. There is beauty and potential everywhere.

8. **Purpose:** This is about a clarity of purpose, values and vision. Everyone can explain how their role aligns to the strategic plan and priorities of the school. It is about doing the right work the right way.

9. **Exactitude:** People like behaviour to be consistent and true. They expect the leader to be fair and ethical. They look for justice.

10. **Expectation:** Humans feel safe if they have a sense of clarity around what to expect. You can't always provide certainty as things change, but you can provide clarity.

My disappointment or joy may not match yours

One important caveat to consider in regard to human needs is that for one person an event will be felt differently than for another, depending on their personal priority of needs. For example, if I say I am hugely disappointed that I didn't get that promotion, I may actually mean a disappointment score of 4 on a scale of 1–10 (10 being not coping and 1 being totally don't care), whereas someone else could say the same thing and mean a disappointment score of 9. It is not about the words they use, it is about the level of need and depth of feeling. Therefore, be mindful of projection. Projection is when you tell your son to put on a jumper because *you* feel cold!

Differentiate for different people

Given we have different needs with different levels of intensity, because we have different brain maps, an influential leader personalises the way they communicate and connect with individuals to bring out their best selves. Charlie Moncada, a principal and former business leader, is a school improvement coach. Charlie's success speaks volumes in regard to his ability to resonate with others through factoring in human needs. His focus on getting to know his people and understanding their perspectives in order to provide them with what they need to be successful is reflected in his ability to unite a team. He states that, 'We have the ability to differentiate and lead people in different ways dependent on needs, experience, personality types and skill, rather than a one-size-fits-all model of leadership. Perspective and differentiation are a direct and highly valuable by-product of being connected to your team.'

> ### Reflective questions
> - Can you identify and compare Maslow's hierarchy with the ESCAPE model. What is the difference? What does this difference mean for your leadership influence?
> - What is the most important motivational trigger for you at work?

- Can you map the team's motivational needs? Is everyone meeting their human needs, and if not what does this mean for team performance?
- What does comfort look like at work?
- What would people say if you asked them to tell you about the things that make their job unnecessarily hard?

F IS FOR FORTITUDE AND BOUNDARIES

'Structures shape desired behaviours.'
Dr Pete Stebbins

Without boundaries anything goes

A powerful way to shape desired behaviour is to modify the decision-making environment, making it more likely that people will choose a certain option. This is called 'choice architecture' and it uses priming and options to influence people's choices. The term 'choice architecture' was first coined by Richard Thaler and Cass Sunstein in their book *Nudge* (2022). It does not involve coercion but nudges people towards a particular decision or outcome.

If you extend this thinking by understanding that we can only control our own behaviour (Glasser, 1998), meaning that we can't control other people, it makes sense to embed structures that shape desired behaviours.

Strategies using this philosophy include:

- Using preset defaults
- Presenting options so one is more favourable
- Using priming to impact on thinking
- Embedding structures that shape behaviour.

Structures that shape desired behaviours examples are:

- Accountability chart
- Meeting agenda design
- Signage
- Meeting protocols.

Hold your ground

Fortitude is about taking courage in discomfort. It is about holding your ground and standing firm when the wind might blow you over or you are swimming against the current. It might be about:

- Having the courage to speak up to say what is right when you know there will be aggressive resistance
- Resolving to lean into a challenge when things are uncertain
- Staying calm when everyone else around you is going crazy in a very stressful event
- Pitching an idea that pushes the boundaries to cut through the bureaucracy.

Reflective questions

- How can you apply choice architecture in your school to shape desired behaviours?
- What issue comes to mind when you think about strengthening your boundaries?
- Does your meeting agenda design use time well?
- Can you think of a situation where it would be helpful to understand that you can only control your own behaviour?
- Think of something you want to do but have not got time to do. Who are you going to disappoint, and can you live with their disapproval?

L IS FOR LEADERSHIP STRENGTH

Sometimes you get what you ask for

Leaders of influence have an inner strength that inspires others to want to listen and work with them. Yet, our brain's first instinct is to keep us safe, so we have a tendency to play small. We are wired to avoid the loss in change. Sometimes we need to lean into a challenge and ignore our fear. We also need to attend to the fear in others when we introduce a big idea that pushes the boundaries. Think about your true purpose. Leaders have a firm grasp on the concept of leadership and form a personal yardstick of what leadership means to them and where they will invest their effort and time. Carve off your first big idea and ask for what you want.

Sometimes we get what we ask for. Sell the benefits, paint a clear vision, be positive about everyone involved so they want to be associated with your idea, address any fears they have and you may find that others want to be part of that success too. Lean into the discomfort of change and push into resistance, as that is where the learning occurs.

Can you live with the disapproval of others?

Leaders are watched and judged. People only praise or blame; they don't always take the time to fully understand. This means that a leader needs to build internal strength, as they can't keep everyone happy all the time. In fact, everyone will want a piece of you. Parents will want you to turn up for a long parent and citizen, board or school council meeting; students will want to show you their work; teachers will want to share their stories and concerns; and citizens will want to tell you about how they see your school doing. If you can't keep everyone happy (and you can't always do that), you need to ask yourself who you are going to disappoint today and whether you can live with the discomfort of their disapproval (Stebbins, 2015). This is a part of leadership. You need to anchor into cast-iron values for decisions, not get blown down by the first puff of wind or lose sleep over everyone's opinion. You can't always share all the information you have, and not everyone has been privy to all the conversations and consultation that led up to a decision. You need to use your time wisely, and it is helpful to think of time as a strong mindset. For this reason, you may find the time tool helpful.

It starts with me: The 'them and us' mindset

Quite often, leadership problems don't lie with the team but are inherent in the leader. These issues are amplified when you are leading without positional authority. Korn Ferry (n.d.) reported that approximately 72 per cent of leaders stated that their roles require them to influence others without having formal authority over them. This finding underscores the changing nature of leadership, where success depends on the ability to build trust and relationships to unite for an 'all-in approach' rather than a 'them and us' mindset. This shift calls for leaders to establish a toolkit of persuasion tools, strengthen their own inner resilience and develop a deep understanding of emotional intelligence. How you lead with influence, even without the positional authority, is shown in the DISCO framework.

D	**Draw** a line in the sand: Anchor into a place of certainty. This is, values, purpose, safety, standards, rules, and evidence rather than the loudest voice.
I	**Influence** mastery: Inspire (brain 1), connect (brain 2), and clarity (brain 3). These neural pathways are interrelated to build trust, rapport and credibility. Cognition and emotion can't be separated, so how we feel about someone will determine our willingness to engage. Reduce the tendency towards a 'them and us' mindset. Inspire, unite and deliver for an all-in approach.
S	**Structures** shape desired behaviours: You can't influence by personality alone. Modify the decision-making environment. Create settings where people are more likely to and can more easily make certain choices.

C	**Composure:** Know your triggers. Learn calming techniques so that you can access your prefrontal cortex for problem-solving and critical thinking. Don't allow your response to become part of the problem. You don't have to win or be right all the time. You don't have to buy into every comment made.
O	**Ownership:** Take action yourself rather than wait for other people's validation or permission. You can only control your own behaviour. You can't control other people's mood, behaviour or opinions. Other people don't have any power over you unless you give them that power. None of your self-esteem is invested in what someone thinks of you unless you let it. You won't please everyone, so ask yourself who you are going to disappoint today and whether you can live with the discomfort of their disapproval. Don't allow yourself to be blown around by other people's choices.

Table 34: The DISCO framework

Time management is a mindset

If you never get to the bottom of your inbox, and arrive at the end of the week feeling like you haven't got anything done, you are not alone. Leaders often try to solve every problem and keep on top of every detail so they feel they have their finger on the pulse, but this can wear you out and keep you away from the important work. An influential leader only works on what leaders can do. They share their thinking about criteria and purpose so that others can be empowered to lead and make the decisions. They don't just delegate, they build other leaders. Think of these as time hacks.

1. Focus on what you can influence, as you can only control your own behaviour. Resist the brain's tendency to focus on all the things you are concerned about.
2. Accept that there is always going to be more work than you can get done. Adjust your expectations; otherwise, you will always feel overwhelmed, disappointed or worse, incompetent.
3. Next time you think 'I haven't got time for that', substitute 'It's not really important to me.'
4. Learn to say no. Establish strong boundaries. When you prioritise or say no, tell yourself it is okay to live with the discomfort of the disapproval. This requires a leader to know what they should be doing.

5. Do the scariest jobs first, as Brian Tracy suggests in his book *Eat That Frog!* (2017).
6. Is everyone doing their bit? 'If each of us would only sweep our own doorstep, the whole world would be clean' (Mother Teresa).
7. Identify who owns the problem. 'Get the monkey off your back' (Ken Blanchard et al., 2000).
8. Stay with the struggle. Some things take new learning and unlearning in order to get them done. This takes effort.
9. Put the big rocks in first. Do the important things first; otherwise, you won't fit them in around the sand. Align your energy and time to your purpose and vision.
10. Consider that if you have more than a few priorities, perhaps you haven't got any priorities.
11. Make time for the proactive strategic leadership work for continued improvement so your school moves forward. It is easy to get seduced by the operational management work, as it is faster, more comfortable and safer.
12. Make good decisions. Are your decisions anchored into your priorities, values, integrity, purpose and evidence? Or do you make your decisions based on recent events, which way the wind is blowing, or the loudest voice?
13. Filter what comes down from above.
14. Ask for what you want: you might just get it.
15. Share your thinking as you make decisions so that others can start making the sound decisions you would make yourself.

Strong leaders are self-disciplined

It makes sense that to increase your influence as a leader you want to be seen as a good role model. One topic that is often raised among leadership groups is the habits we form around our own wellbeing. All school leaders are very busy and many tell me they find making time for exercise and other wellbeing habits very challenging. This is made harder by the fact that our brain was designed to move, connect and problem-solve, yet we live in a world of convenience, isolation and comfort. We have remote controls for our television, Uber Eats, vacuum cleaners, shopping centres, cars – and the list goes on. The neuroscientists generally agree that wellbeing habits include exercise, quality nutrition, sound sleep, connection to others and anti-stress strategies, to name but a few.

Project confidence

Leaders show strength by projecting confidence but not arrogance. These things can help to give you a confident vibe:

- Hold your posture and make eye contact.
- Learn the correct grammar and table manners.
- Show warmth and curiosity.
- Own your space: don't let people interrupt. 'I like your idea but I haven't outlined my thinking yet.'
- Natural is elegant.
- Drop word fillers such as 'um', 'right'.
- Drop word qualifiers such as 'I may be wrong but...'
- Project yourself in the role. Dress and sound like what you want to be tomorrow.
- Fight fair: 'I have a different perspective on that and...'
- Maintain your composure.
- Ask questions to break tension rather than point the finger.
- Don't argue with an idiot, because they are better at it.

> *'I am torn between correcting grammar and table manners and wanting friends!'*
>
> Anon.

Reflective questions

- What strategies can you apply to use your time more effectively?
- How do you define leadership? What does this mean for your behaviours?
- What goals have you set around wellbeing, and how would you rate your self-discipline?
- How can you enhance the way you project confidence?
- How would you rate your confidence level with establishing an all-in culture to reduce the 'them and us' mindset?

U IS FOR UNDERSTANDING BIAS

'If you can't anchor into a place of certainty or a combination of evidence and a long-lived experience of expertise, you must be relying on opinion, bias and shooting from the hip.'
Dr Judi Newman

In his book *Strangers to Ourselves: Discovering the Adaptive Unconscious* (2002), Wilson references an estimate that the human brain processes approximately 11 million bits of information per second, but we are only consciously aware of about 40 to 50 bits per second. The short-term memory can only remember about three pieces of information and one complex piece. So, it is not surprising that the brain uses shortcuts, as it cannot process all the information coming in.

The brain thinks in expectation and attempts to continually predict what is going to happen based on prior wiring to prepare us for the future. We therefore see things according to our expectations and can often get a lot wrong. The brain likes to save fuel and instinctively uses hardwired neural pathways so our reality and world view are firmly set in place. We have defence mechanisms to ensure the world stays the way we expect it to be. These shortcuts in thinking are called cognitive bias. A cognitive bias is anything that distorts your thinking away from a point of truth. Table 35 outlines a number of the more well-documented cognitive biases.

Cognitive bias	Description
Confirmation bias	When you only look for information that confirms your existing beliefs.
Cherry picking	When only a specific piece of information is selected to explain your reasoning and you ignore the rest.
Black and white	Thinking only in terms of one extreme or another – all bad or all good – ignoring the grey areas.
Intergroup bias	This is also called the 'them and us' mindset: when you favour those who are part of your group and view others with suspicion or less empathy.
Personalising	Arguing against an issue because you don't like the person who is delivering the message.
Projecting	Arguing against something because it unconsciously reflects something you fear yourself but may in fact be quite reasonable for another person.
White coat syndrome	Being anxious and shaping your response differently around a professional or someone in authority.
Popularity bias	Appealing to emotion based on what is popular to other people. Thinking that if everyone likes it, it must be good or right.
Gender bias	Distorted thinking based on someone's gender.
Poisoning the well	Being so committed to a position that you are blind to reason, no matter what facts are presented.
Incentive bias	When extrinsic rewards are provided as a motivator and they have the opposite effect.
Herd mentality	Also called group bias. When people blindly go along with what others are doing without questioning the decision.
Loss aversion	A tendency to fear loss more than seeing it as an opportunity for gain.
Framing	When someone makes a decision based on how the information was presented to them.
Anchoring bias	Taking pre-existing data as a reference point for all subsequent data, which can skew decision-making. When we rely on the first information we are given.
IKEA effect	We place more value on things we help create.

Cognitive bias	Description
Hyperbolic discounting	A tendency to value immediate rewards over long-term rewards.
Self-serving bias	Blaming external factors for personal errors.
Illusory truth effect	We are more likely to believe misinformation when it is repeated.
Dunning-Kruger effect	We think we are better than we really are when our skill level or knowledge is low.
Availability heuristic	Tendency to think that things that happened recently are more likely to happen again.
Decision bias	Why we make worse decisions at the end of the day.
Affect heuristic	When we rely on current emotions to make decisions.
Halo effect	When we apply a positive importance based on a positive attitude in another area.
Lego effect	Adults are more likely to add rather than take away when problem-solving.
Sensitisation	When something is repeated so often that you overreact to it.
Habituation	When something is repeated so often that you don't notice it anymore.

Table 35: Cognitive bias

Understand habituation and sensitisation

Habituation is when something is repeated so often that you don't notice it anymore, and sensitisation is when it is repeated so often that you overreact. This is a story that illustrates this bias.

Jeffery Dahmer, a well-documented serial killer in the USA, killed people and chopped them up, hiding them in his deep freezer. He lived with his elderly grandmother in her basement. She knew he brought friends home, as the noise kept her awake. Eventually, she slept through the noise (this is habituation) as she didn't notice it anymore. One night, screams woke her up in the small hours of the night, and she kicked Jeffery out (this is sensitisation). Months later, they resolved their differences and he moved back in. The police were in the neighbourhood and saw a naked boy running from the house. They took him back to the house because he was a Mexican who could not speak English and they could not understand him. Jeffery convinced the police they had had a lovers' tiff. Even though the police could smell something bad coming out of the house, they brushed it off because the neighbourhood was in poor condition and smelt (this is habituation). The boy was never seen again. He was only 14. Jeffery got away with killing 17 people before he was caught.

Anchoring can distort decision-making

Kahneman (2011) and a colleague ran an experiment that showed the power of anchoring to distort thinking. Participants were asked to estimate the percentage of African countries in the United Nations. The researchers showed one group the number 10 and asked, 'Is the percentage higher or lower than 10 per cent?' then asked them to make an estimation of the true percentage. Next, they showed another group the number 65 and asked them, 'Is the percentage higher or lower than 65 per cent?' then asked them to make an estimation of the true percentage. Even though the number they were shown had no connection to the correct answer, participants' thinking was influenced by the anchor, meaning that the first group responded with lower guesses and the second group responded with higher guesses. The anchor distorted the decision-making process, making the participants rely on the initial information as a reference point rather than consider all the information.

Adults have a tendency to add rather than subtract

Folklore has it that a father and son were building a bridge out of Lego and part of the bridge collapsed. The father collected more Lego bricks to fix the problem, and in the time it took for the father to do that, the young son had fixed the problem by removing some of the bricks in the design. Adults tend to have a bias towards adding as opposed to subtracting when faced with complex problem-solving (Adams, 2021). This is called the Lego bias.

In a study by Levine and Murnane (2012), participants were tasked with solving a problem that involved simplifying an already complex situation. Despite the fact that the optimal solution was to subtract elements from the problem, participants were more likely to add new ideas or features. This bias towards adding rather than subtracting leads to overcomplication of solutions, even when simplicity might yield better results.

This bias is seen not only in design contexts (like Lego construction or product design) but also in areas like policy-making, business strategy, and even personal life, where people may add commitments, obligations or activities, instead of cutting back on those that are less useful or necessary.

> *'If the only tool you have is a hammer,*
> *you tend to see every problem as a nail.'*
> Alfred Adler

See what others don't see

If a leader has a deep understanding of the different types of cognitive bias (some of which are shown in Table 35) and accepts that we all have them, they may be able to see what is really happening despite what others may say. When something is said that sounds logical but doesn't sound quite right, question the underlying premise. Ask yourself, 'What am I missing here? How do others read this situation? Are my feelings and beliefs getting in the way?'

> *'We can be blind to the obvious,*
> *and we are also blind to our blindness.'*
> Daniel Kahneman

Reflective questions

- What bias can be relevant to your work as a leader or teacher? Can you give examples?
- Can you think about how the Lego effect relates to leadership?
- Have you experienced sensitisation or habituation?
- When have you felt the IKEA effect?
- Can you think of an example of the Dunning-Kruger effect?

- Have you ever seen the availability bias affect motivational behaviour in your team?
- What other implications can you see in relation to leadership practice?
- How can you use this information to help you see around corners and see what others can't see?

E IS FOR EMOTION

*'Sustained change only happens when we shift
at an emotional level rather than a logical level.'*
Robin Sharma

Emotion is at the very heart of motivation because it can draw attention and galvanise positive action. Good influencers know how to connect with people's hopes, fears, identity and values. It is widely held that there are six universal emotions: anger, sadness, fear, disgust, surprise and happiness. Additionally, there are over 500 feelings, such as inspired, frustrated, hopeful and proud. Emotions are the initial neurological response, and feelings are the effect, being the slower psychological response. For the purpose of this book, I use the term emotion as a general term for both emotions and feelings.

Humans are not wired to react dispassionately to information (Boyatzis, 2012; Feser, 2016; Gordon, 2022; Wang 2019). As humans, we attach our feeling to what we think about and this emotional connection determines how we respond (Gordon, 2022; Kennedy, 2021). If leaders can harness emotion by addressing human feelings, such as desire and fear, rather than just focusing on the facts, they can strengthen their impact. Relying only on logic and data to persuade is not always enough. Telling stories to create an emotional response will be more memorable and therefore more influential. For example, you can tell a small child not to touch the hotplate. They understand the meaning of the words and comprehend that a hotplate heats up. However, if they touch it when it is on, they will never touch it again. They have experienced pain and an associated emotion, triggering a change in thinking and new behaviour.

Delegate the inconvenience

Mum was in her late eighties, a widow living alone, with early-stage dementia setting in. I was frequently flying in and out for work, so I arranged for carers to support her. One visited each morning to help her start the day, supervising her medication, doing her laundry, and taking her to social activities. Another came in the evening to assist with dinner and ensure she was safe for the night. Mum was determined to remain in her own home, the place where she'd spent most of her married life, for as long as possible. Her quiet stoicism was something I deeply admired.

As her short-term memory declined, I installed a small safe for her medication; otherwise, she would take it multiple times. It was the carer's responsibility to ensure she took it correctly and to refill prescriptions every fortnight. One day, during a visit, I discovered she'd run out of her medication – the prescription hadn't been filled. At 8 pm, I drove around looking for a 24-hour chemist, managed to get it filled, and made sure everything was ready for the following day. I called the agency to report the issue. They apologised and assured me it wouldn't happen again.

A month later, I found the safe empty once more and had to fill the script myself. This time, I contacted the team leader and asked what strategies were in place to make sure it didn't keep happening. She assured me that she'd noted the issue and would send a memo to all case workers. Three months passed, and then it happened again.

This time, I visited the agency manager in person. I explained the recurring problem and offered some practical solutions. She was professional, apologetic and receptive. But when the same thing happened yet again, I decided to take a different approach. I deliberately left the safe empty, placing a note inside that read, 'Margaret has run out of medication.' I knew the next carer wouldn't be able to solve the issue on the spot, as they had another client to get to. As expected, the missing medication set off a chain of conversations among the team reaching the team boss. It never happened again. Why? Because I had delegated the inconvenience.

Sometimes, logic alone isn't enough to change behaviour. People need to feel the impact of a problem before they're motivated to fix it. When the burden was shared, real change occurred.

Have a koala moment

Sally was an advocate of saving the koala population, as she had read that many of our koala colonies are on the decline from bush fires, road accidents, wild dog attacks and the removal of trees for housing developments. However, it wasn't until she cared for a tiny baby koala who had lost its mother to the bush fires that Sally became an active champion of the koala campaign, her intent taking on new meaning. She came to love that sensitive intelligent warm furry creature. He hung from the curtains in her living room and would hold tightly onto her thick jumper. He never scratched or bit her. When Sally released that koala back into the wild, she was emotionally invested and wanted to do everything that she could to protect that beautiful creature she had come to know and understand. Sally now had 'skin in the game' – a powerful influence tactic.

Cold hard decisions

Emotion is so closely entwined with the decisions we make that you would think that if we lost the key parts of our brain that controlled emotional processing we would be better able to make cold hard logical decisions. However, that is not the case. Elliot was a manager, husband and father. He had a brain tumour removed from his frontal lobe. After surgery, he experienced a profound change in his ability to feel emotions, although his intelligence and memory were intact. The neuroscientist Antonio Damasio studied the case and found that Elliot could not make a decision post-surgery. He had difficulty in choosing what to eat for breakfast, what to wear and all other decisions that were a normal part of his day. He could no longer hold down his company role. Damasio's conclusion was that emotion is important to decision-making. This case is detailed in Damasio's book *Descartes' Error: Emotion, Reason, and the Human Brain* (1994).

I like inferior shampoo

Dempsey and Mitchell carried out an experiment that provided evidence-based information about the effectiveness of products such as shampoo and soap. Despite the research data contradicting their habitual choices, the participants still preferred the soap and shampoo they now knew were inferior. This is another example showing that logic and data are not always enough to change thinking. People unconsciously prioritise emotional information in decision-making; their subjective feelings influence their behaviour over their objective thinking. We overweigh personal testimonials and stories and are less impressed by statistics (Kahneman, 2011). We need time to rewire our brains to change our thinking for new behaviours. We have to make our own connections according to our available neural hardwiring. If we are not given time to reflect and process the new information, with sleep in between and repeated exposure, we can't create the new wiring. Supporting people through change and helping them come to terms with what they may lose is important because that part of them has served them in some way and now feels like it is missing. Don't dismiss emotion. It is a game changer.

Embrace the magic three

As emotions are so essential to our ability to influence, another way to influence is to embrace the 'magic three'. If you want to make an impression on someone, there are three conditions that can make the interaction more influential. I call them the magic three because your brain is able to capture three concepts well:

1. Make a positive connection: studies show that people remember a positive interaction as it reveals emotion.
2. Create an experience tapping into emotion: give them a story to tell.
3. Appeal to their status: studies show that humans like to feel significant and valued, an emotional response.

Reflective questions

- How could you create the magic three to make your next interaction memorable?
- How many koala moments do you create at school or in the classroom?
- Can you think of a way you can delegate the inconvenience with a persistent problem you have tried to solve with logic?

N IS FOR NEUROPLASTICITY

'Thinking is difficult, that's why most people judge.'
Carl Jung

Allow time for the brain to rewire

In order to influence others, a leader needs to be able to change thinking for new behaviours. There is limited behaviour change without neuroplastic changes in the brain over time (Gordon, 2022). The brain requires time to rewire, so incorporate a series of conversations with sleep in between. Not many changes happen in one conversation. View aspiring leaders as unfinished work as they are in their formative years. They need to be able to make mistakes. See people for their potential not their current story.

Humans also need to be supported through change as the brain rewires. Change means different things for different people, and some will need more support than others. For some individuals, it may take some time to change belief systems and priorities as the brain rewires. For others, it might just involve new training and updated resources. Either way, a school principal will benefit from understanding the change process and having a plan to move people through the change phase that aligns with how the brain operates. In her book *On Death and Dying*, Elisabeth Kübler-Ross (1969) describes the emotional stages of the terminally ill as denial, anger, bargaining, depression and acceptance. It has been suggested that the stages of change have been linked to these brain states.

Neuroplastic changes when we learn

Thinking and feeling start in the brain, with cognition being an emotional process (Immordino-Yang, 2016; Gordon, 2022). As we learn over time, the neuroplastic changes incorporate thickening of the myelin, strengthening of the synapse, branching of dendrites, development of spines, and more efficient receptors. Every time a thought, feeling or action is repeated, the synaptic connection between neurons is strengthened, making it more efficient (Gluck et al., 2016; Gordon, 2022; Medina, 2008; Whitman & Kelleher, 2016). A neuron is shown in Figure 11.

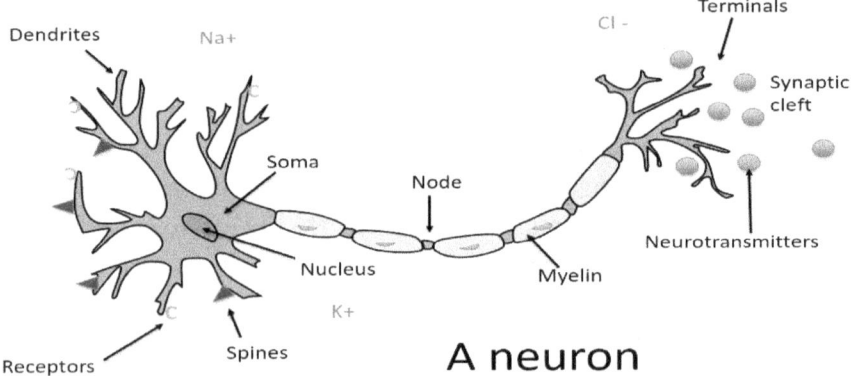

Figure: 11: A neuron

Change leadership

Schools are places of continuous change. Humans are anxious when change is approaching. So, the influential leader brings people through change by minimising the stress that it can bring and preparing the way.

DANCER is a six-step change-management process that aligns with how the brain operates to support teams through change (see Table 36). Change is like a dancer. It moves and adapts to the tune you are playing.

D	Desire	Build curiosity and desire through painting a picture of a compelling vision. Sell the benefits of a preferred future.
A	Allow	Allow a voice and time to learn to rewire the brain. Listen, mine for beliefs and remove barriers. Take away the fear.
N	New	Immerse in a new stimulating experience and embed structures that shape desired new behaviours. Invite participation and aim for all-in. If it is compelling and attractive, people will want to sign up rather than feel mandated.
C	Conversations	Focus on direct conversations with individuals and groups. Help others through the grieving process.
E	Execute	Execute and reward the behaviour you want to see. Reinforce optimism. Encourage potential. You might start with the enthusiastic. Stay flexible and adapt as required.
R	Refine	Celebrate wins, polish, fine-tune and adapt. Stay flexible.

Table 36: The DANCER change-management process

How do we learn?

To influence another human is to learn new thinking or behaviour, but what does the brain require for learning to take place? Learning is closing the gap between what we know already and updating our mental maps for continuous improvement. Nine conditions are required to bring about the neuroplastic changes that consolidate memory. If you can't remember it, you haven't learnt it. The 'Learn the dream' framework in Table 37 illustrates how we learn.

D	Downtime	The brain requires an incubating period after learning, to encode the data. Encoding is about strengthening the neural connections, developing spines as part of the neuroplastic changes. This is processing time, which is different from a brain break to reduce cognitive load.
R	Recall	If you can't recall it, you haven't learnt it. It is essential to learn over time with sleep in between to provide time for reflection, retrieval, repetition and rewiring.

E	Effort	Learning is an effortful process, not a passive activity. If you don't invest effort, then you don't strengthen the neural pathways.
	Emotion	Emotion holds your interest as curiosity and motivation spike. Positive emotion soaks dendrites in neurotransmitters and hormones that enable them to branch and strengthen.
	Error detection	Address the gap between what we know (our current wiring) and what we come to understand. To learn is to update and improve our wiring.
A	Application	If you can't apply it, you don't understand it and you won't be able to use it. The brain is context- and state-sensitive, so apply the new learning to different contexts to consolidate.
	Attention	You only remember what you pay attention to. You have 30 seconds to hook the attention of the learner. Practising focus and concentration will help improve learning.
M	Meaning	If it is not meaningful, it won't link to prior learning and may be stored in a remote part of the brain, making retrieval tricky.
	Modality	The more areas of the brain that are used when learning, the more pathways are created, making learning more effective. Using a range of modes in teaching will use multisensory pathways. Teach the concept in different ways: Write it, read it, hear it, discuss it, draw it, act it out, question it, analyse it.

Table 37: Learn the dream

At the next staff meeting, think about how you are influencing change and if the 'Learn the dream' factors are embedded in your address or presentation. I have witnessed some brilliant school speakers and have seen this play out with outstanding results. Additionally, walk around the classrooms and notice how many of the ingredients in the DREAM are evident in the pedagogy. What is missing? What impact does this have? How can it be improved? Did the masterful lesson where every child is engaged and learning have all the ingredients? How do you know?

Endorse an experience of high impact

The brain chemicals have a significant role in the way we learn, feel and behave. Strengthen your influence on the wellness, performance and motivation of others by creating an event that incorporates the following:

- Shared joyful new experience
- Emotional connections
- Story to tell
- Status-building
- Soft curves and sunshine
- Outdoors and movement
- Creativity
- Purpose and achievement.

Why? This scenario triggers the release of a number of key neurotransmitters and hormones that have a combined role in motivation, mood, masking pain and contentment. The ENDORSE model is outlined in Table 38. Endorse an experience of high impact.

E	Endorphins	A neurotransmitter that masks pain and promotes euphoria for improved wellbeing and stress resilience. (exercise, laughter, creativity, challenge, achievement)
N	Norepinephrine	High release equals heightened arousal and improves ability to handle stress. (exercise, fresh foods, sunlight exposure)
D	Dopamine	Plays a role in the brain's reward system but is also associated with motivation, pleasure and learning. (achieve a goal, exercise, receiving praise, winning, laughter, new experiences)
O	Oxytocin	Plays a role in social bonding and emotional connection. (hug, group loyalty, trust, cooperation, memorable moment)
R	Reduce cortisol	Released to increase our alertness and focus to fight or flight. Makes us feel stressed. (to reduce cortisol, exercise, rest and wilderness experiences)

S	Serotonin	Regulates mood and behaviour, especially in regard to wellbeing. High levels associated with feeling content and low levels with mood disorders such as depression. Impacts on our confidence levels. (pride, exposure to sunlight, helping others, outdoors)
E	Endocannabinoids	Associated with wellbeing and motivation. Reduces stress and anxiety. (exercise, fresh foods, sleep, destressing, touch, connection, laughter)

Table 38: The ENDORSE model

What event could capture the ENDORSE factors?

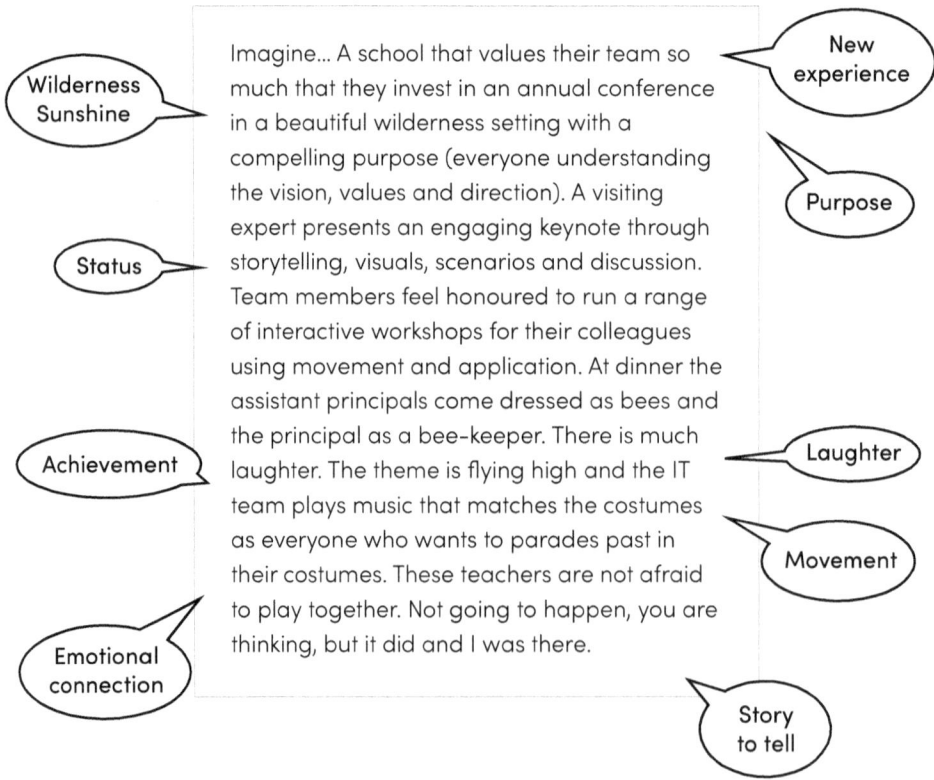

Adult learners

When studying neuroplasticity, we need to be mindful of how adults learn. The adult brain has many more neural changes in its long-term memory called schemas. Therefore, when adults learn something new, they can make more connections and experience less cognitive load. On the other hand, the adult brain schemas may also block new learning, as sometimes we have to unlearn to relearn. Research has shown that adults retain learning and grow when the learning experience:

- Has real-life application
- Is relevant now
- Is clear and compact
- Is supported by evidence and research
- Is applied and adapted quickly
- Is connected to what we already know
- Is revisited and deepened over time
- Is shared and discussed with others
- Has narrative and a visual-driven delivery.

The rewire conversation

When a student or teacher has an inappropriate or unhelpful reaction, telling them what to do often just makes them more defensive. In particular, confrontation rarely works on teenagers, and it doesn't teach young people how to self-manage. One way to rewire the brain is to use the REWIRE conversation (see Table 39). The REWIRE conversation teaches the child the power to choose, improve responses and control, and take responsibility for their actions.

R	React	How did you react?
E	Emotion	How did you feel? (shows empathy)
W	Wise	Was the consequence helpful?
I	Improve	What is a better way to respond?
R	Reflect	What are you going to do?
E	Encourage	How can I support that decision?

Table 39: The REWIRE conversation

Reflective questions

- When was the last time you were involved in significant change and how did you feel? Were you anxious about what you had to lose?
- How do you know you are working on essential meaningful change in your school rather than just reorganising the deck chairs?
- When you run staff professional development, how to do you incorporate the DREAM factors?
- How could you maximise your impact using the ENDORSE model?

T IS FOR TRADITION AND CULTURE

'If you want to build a ship, don't herd people together to collect wood and don't assign them tasks and work but rather teach them to long for the endless immensity of the sea.'
Antoine de Saint-Exupéry

Experience not programs

The first employee experience should be reflected in the induction program. It should build inspiration, unity and connection on the first day. It is not just a checklist or introductions but provides the foundations to build confidence, pride and capability levels in adopting the new workplace expectations, traditions and culture. If the workday is felt, it becomes part of the culture. It is not about adding programs, strategies or giving out free pens. The school culture is more about the leaders of the school jumping into conversations, asking what makes the work harder than it needs to be and moving from managing to connecting (Schwantes, 2025). Another important element of school culture is establishing traditions that are unique to the school.

Start with yourself

As they say, a fish stinks from the head down, so if you want to change the workplace culture you need to start with yourself and the senior leadership team. You can be the hardest-working or smartest person in the room, but if you are not self-aware and working on improving yourself, everything else will come undone. Culture is not just what you do but also what you allow, endorse or ignore. Culture is created by what leaders tolerate.

My experience in schools has led me to believe that continuous change for improvement to a school culture is very doable but is not a linear process. It reminds me of a trophic cascade effect (see next paragraph). If you start with yourself, one improvement is linked to another, as the school culture is an invisible web of connections. Continuous improvement will have an exponential effect, resulting in independent autonomous collaborative responses.

Yellowstone National Park

Shifting and transforming workplace culture must begin with the top: the principal. It is a messy, non-transferrable process and deeply context-dependent: What works for one school may not work for another. A trophic cascade is a process of change from the top of the food chain with a flow-on effect to the bottom. A compelling example is the story of Yellowstone National Park.

At the turn of the century, the grey wolves were eliminated by hunters, triggering a decline of the park's eco-system balance. Without their natural predators, the elk population exploded, growing to 20,000. The willow and aspen trees were over-grazed, and the harsh hooves of the elk muddied the riverbanks, impeding the river's flow.

In 1995, 41 grey wolves were reintroduced, transforming the park as the elk and deer were reduced. The willows and aspens flourished once again, stabilising the riverbanks. The elk and deer no longer lingered around the water's edge, because they didn't want to be attacked by wolves. The rivers recovered and the beavers returned, building their dams and raising the water table, awakening the dormant seeds. The trees grew taller and stronger, creating shade and deep roots. Moose, bison, foxes, coyotes, squirrels, badgers, flowers, bees and insects were restored, transforming the entire eco-system.

This story is a reminder that we need to fix the top level first and that one improvement is linked to another. Leadership sets the conditions for transformation. When the foundation is healthy, each improvement gives rise to another, rippling throughout the organisation.

A cultural belief may be stronger than a scientific truth

When I arrived at a secondary school as principal, I noticed that of the students who were failing both physics and the higher maths subjects in Year 11, 100 per cent had failed Year 10 maths. Most of these students did not recover, even after they changed to an easier maths subject, despite tutoring, due to the loss of sequential time in maths and a damaged self-belief.

I asked why the students were allowed to choose subjects too difficult for them without support and suggested we were setting them up to fail. I shared the data. I advocated for a different approach to help these students realise their dreams. A year later, nothing much had changed. It then occurred to me that this was not a simple structural problem; it was a cultural problem that was embedded in the school community's belief system by parents and teachers, based on the desire to delay specialisation for our young people and not lock them into one pathway too soon. This culture developed with the best of intentions but was not helping our students to reach their potential. I needed to address the feelings behind that belief before things would change. As Peter Drucker says, 'Culture eats strategy for breakfast.'

Culture shapes behaviour

An empirical study by Edgar Schein (2010), an organisational psychologist, showed that culture (shared beliefs, values and norms) shapes behaviour and performance in organisations. He concluded that culture is essential in driving organisational success and found that:

- In workplaces where the goals and strategies matched the culture, performance and morale was higher.
- Behaviour expectations and social norms will impact on the culture. For example, if there is low trust and fear, performance will decline. If there is high trust and transparency, performance will rise.
- Leaders need to role-model the behaviour they want to see to set the tone and standards of behaviour. A workplace culture that is toxic will affect every person in the organisation and change will be very difficult.

- Individuals are more likely to be motivated when they feel the workplace culture meets their needs and values. If a team member desires autonomy and connection and the workplace supports those needs in the way it does business, then job satisfaction and engagement increase.

Traditions reinforce culture

When assessing the workplace culture, consider the impact of the traditions in the system levels, from nano to supra level, shown in Table 40. If there is misalignment, a problem may show up in the school culture.

Level	School leadership example
Nano	Classroom level
Micro	Subject department level
Meso	Principal level
Macro	Whole school community level
Supra	Department of Education level

Table 40: System levels

Reflective questions

- What is your school plan for shifting or improving your workplace culture?
- How do you know what culture you have?
- Can you name one improvement that has led to many others in your school?
- What long-held traditions do you have at your school to build the culture?

I IS FOR INTENTIONAL CONVERSATIONS

> *'Most conversations are simply a monologue delivered in the presence of a witness.'*
> Margaret Miller

Some sound advice I received from a mentor many years ago was to ensure I had individual conversations with the senior leadership team, not just group discussions. One-to-one conversations raise the stakes, as they allow focused attention on individual needs, provide an opportunity for private feedback, and are more likely to hold others accountable as there is nowhere to hide.

The PPPP conversation

Investing time to meet with team members individually is a popular practice among effective principals. One principal I interviewed used a simple framework to conduct individual conversations based on People, Purpose, Performance and Position, which can guide the conversation and keep both parties on track.

- **People:** How are you travelling? How is your team? (Check in about the wellbeing of the team. Coach the human, not just the content.)
- **Purpose:** Tell me about your success and progress with your priority work? (Keep people accountable and working on the important work.)
- **Performance:** How do you think you are going? Can I give you some feedback on what I have noticed? What resources or training would be helpful to meet your goals? Can you give me feedback on how you

think I am going in the role. (Establish a high-performance learning culture to continually improve.)
- **Position:** My view is that we are travelling well on our writing agenda but have a lot of work to do around our reading agenda. What do you think? (Collaborate for input and reinforce key messages.)

Education requires purposeful conversation

As Nelson Mandela said, 'Education is the most powerful weapon which you can use to change the world.' Don't underestimate the ability of purposeful conversations in training to influence results. Allow people to rewire their brain as they learn new insights to impact on their thinking for changed behaviour.

> ### Reflective questions
> - Do you listen to defend your ground or do you listen to learn?
> - Do you listen to save face, win, be right, control or grasp power or do you listen to understand?
> - Do you make time for intentional individual conversations?

A IS FOR ACCOUNTABILITY

*'Responsibility equals accountability equals ownership.
And a sense of ownership is the most powerful weapon
a team or organisation can have.'*
Pat Summitt

There are a number of ways that a leader can hold people to account. Everyone in the team needs to have clarity around their role and a grasp on what the results might look like if they were successful. We are all leaders but have different accountabilities. The principal has the ultimate accountability. One way of looking at this is that not everyone has the same accountability to say yes to every question. I learnt early in my career to never ask a person to say yes unless they have the authority to do so in the first place.

Everyone has a role in the strategic leadership work and the operational management work, but first the team needs to understand the difference. It is easy to be seduced by the busy work, as it feels safer, faster, easier and more comfortable. This is the operational work of policy, systems, training, finance, facilities, to-do lists, filing, resourcing and curriculum. If we are only invested in this area, we will have very organised departments but we will always be putting out fires because it is the reactive work. Leaders need to pull back and let go a little to lean into the strategic leadership work. This is the proactive work that will move your school forward. It is the challenging work of shifting cultures, building capacity, influencing thinking, changing behaviour, communicating hope, raising the bar, setting the tone, getting to the root cause of problems, turning up, confronting dysfunctional behaviour, coaching others, communicating a clear vision and building trust. You can spend hours on this area of work and not have anything tangible to show for it by the end of the day. Nevertheless, it is the work of the influential leader.

Cascade of imitation

The way things are phrased can make all the difference in regard to accountability. One Year 9 deputy principal (DP) was on her way to Year 9 parade in the assembly hall. She saw some girls running on the pathway and yelled out over the crowd noise. 'Stop running, girls. I am tired of seeing you ignore the rules.' The girls ran off around the corner sharing a little giggle as they disappeared into the sunset. When the DP got to parade, she was hot under the collar and waited for the daily announcements to finish. She then proceeded to give the Year 9 cohort a lecture about arriving late to class and truancy. It clearly wasn't the first time she had given this message to the group. I could see their eyes glaze over, with some students nudging their neighbour with their elbow, indicating 'I want a bit of this action', as she said, 'Over a third of this group has either been late to class or missed over 5 per cent of lessons this term. You need to stop being late to lesson. These are the school rules. Everyone seems to think it is OK to be late to class. I have seen the way you dawdle.' Although she had good intentions, she had just reinforced the behaviour she wanted to eliminate. The brain does not process the negative very easily, and their brains would have picked up the words 'late to class' and 'missed… lessons'. This is called the 'cascade of imitation'. When we make a statement in the negative, we are more likely to influence a rush to the exits (Let's all do it) rather than to change the behaviour. Phrasing words in such a way that they align with the way the brain operates is going to be more helpful. In this case, a better way to manage the behaviour would have been to say, 'At Blue Heights State School, we walk on the paths,' and 'Your attendance matters to us. Every lesson counts.' That way, the students would not have felt like they were being lectured but rather that we are in this together for their benefit.

This may help you understand how the brain works: If I told you not to think about a pink elephant, what would you do? You would think about a pink elephant before you could try not to think about one. This shows how your brain is challenged with processing the negative.

Holding people accountable increases performance

Nobre and Martins (2021), conducted a meta-analysis of how accountability influences performance and decision-making and found that it improved motivation, behaviour and performance. If people knew they were being watched and assessed and held to account, they put in more effort as they worked towards meeting their goals and expectations. Participants tended to make higher-quality decisions because they were more thoughtful and strategic about making good choices. This was shown across education, health and business sectors. Stronger ethical behaviours were also linked to accountability, aligning their decisions with social norms.

Use an accountability chart

One of the most influential tools for keeping everyone in the team accountable is to use an accountability chart. Leadership teams often tell me that the discussion required to set one up has given them clarity around their role and useful information about how their role aligns with the greater strategic plan and the roles of the other senior officers. It also highlights the importance of data.

Ask everyone in the team to consider their work in terms of strategic leadership work versus operational management work. Identify a goal to highlight one important part of their strategic leadership work. This is something in their portfolio where they want to make a difference or improvement. The team then fills in the accountability chart shown in Table 41 according to the following guidelines:

1. **Name:** Every leadership team member is accountable for their own results and has clarity around their role.
2. **Priority area:** Drill down to your two or three school priorities. Identify one priority that aligns to your strategic task.
3. **Problem:** Identify what the problem of practice is. What are the pain points?
4. **Goal:** Identify a stretch goal that represents the strategic work you want to drive and lead. Ensure it is a smart goal so you can measure your progress.

5. **Strategies:** These are four or five high-yield actions. What could you do that will get the biggest results? A strategy is a key action.
6. **Leadership influence:** Identify one word that represents the influence you will have. In what way will you scale up your leadership? E.g. Is your purpose consistency, or momentum, or unity, or ownership, or shared common language or authentic collaboration.
7. **Baseline data:** What is your starting point?
8. **Benchmark data:** Identify a standard that you can compare your progress to. E.g. Australian mean.
9. **Who can help?:** Your role is to drive the leadership initiative, but you don't have to do all the legwork or make all the decisions.
10. **Structures:** Nominate the structures that will help shape desired behaviours. E.g. Meeting times, shared norms, classroom charts, checklists, agenda design, reporting and feedback cycles and so on.
11. **Success criteria:** How will you know you are making progress in 3, 6 and 9 months' time? What will you look for? How will you measure your success?
12. **Desired outcome:** What result do you want? If you were successful, what would be different? What change do you want to see at the end?
13. **Reporting cycle:** At each leadership meeting a team member will be nominated by the principal to present progress. At this time, you report back either green (success), yellow (momentum) or red (no progress). If your report is green, you show evidence of your achievement and the team joins with you to celebrate this milestone. If your report is red, your team can collaborate on the problem of practice, give you feedback and share ideas for improvement. Pool your expertise to come up with something better or new. There is no judgment or big stick.

Name:	
Priority area:	
Problem:	
Goal:	
Strategies:	
Leadership influence:	
Baseline data:	
Benchmark data:	
Who can help?:	
Structures:	
Success criteria:	
Desired outcome:	
Reporting cycle:	

Table 41: The accountability chart

A smart meeting agenda design will save time

Another tool for maximising accountability and shaping desired behaviours is a well-designed meeting agenda. Much time is wasted in inefficient meetings. This is a meeting design that has been modified from Dr Pete Stebbins' work (2015). Each section of the agenda has a purpose.

The sections of the agenda design

1. **Shared norms:** The team works out a list of behaviour expectations. The team can make up their own, but they could include:
   - Confidentiality
   - Debate inside the room
   - Unity outside the room
   - Issues over personalities
   - Say it in the room
   - Participate in good faith.
2. **Chair:** The CEO creates the agenda. The team can put topics on the agenda. The CEO ensures everyone keeps to the shared norms and keeps everyone on track. Once the trust is built in the team, the chair's role could be rotated around the team.
3. **Timer:** Always start the meeting and finish the meeting on time.
4. **Team purpose:** This is fashioned by the team with the guidance of the CEO and represents the one thing that the leadership team can do together that will be much more powerful than if they worked individually. What does the leadership team need to nail first? This will depend on where the team is at in regard to their work together. E.g. To build trust and unity for clarity of purpose or consistency of message to the school community.
5. **Check-in protocol:** A check-in protocol is to mark the start of the meeting. It can have one of the following purposes:
   - Share one success story of the week to set a positive tone for the meeting
   - One person to provide an example of evidence of the team purpose.
6. **Sharp priorities:** The meeting always starts with a discussion on the school priority work. If the school's two priorities are reading

and wellbeing, then the discussion will always be centred on these topics but will be different each week to reflect progress, problems of practice and questions.

7. **CEO space:** The principal has a space in the agenda to say and do anything that they deem relevant. It is purposely not the number one item on the agenda, in order to reduce potential power imbalance.
8. **Strategic agenda:** These are topics that are in the strategic area of work such as building capacity, vision, change and new developments.
9. **Operational agenda:** The operational topics are put on last so that the whole meeting is not taken up with minor operational issues that can be dealt with in another way.
10. **HOT issues:** This is the time put aside for team members to raise issues that are a problem or a risk. It is not important to solve the problem at the meeting. The objective is to raise and air issues so that they can be addressed later. A protocol works well for this section.
11. **Professional development reading:** High-performance teams learn together. Either a nominated team member can provide an executive summary of a reading for the group or the group can agree to read a chapter of a book and discuss it each week.
12. **Check-out protocol:** The chair reinforces what has been decided at the meeting and demonstrates how the new information can be framed back in the staffroom. This ensures the same message is released and reduces communication confusion.
13. **Communiqué:** This is not the minutes. The minutes are written on the agenda by a nominated person and filed. A communiqué is a short sharp message that you want the whole school community to see. It might be emailed out or it could be part of the principal's weekly newsletter.

The parts of the meeting agenda are shown in Figure 12.

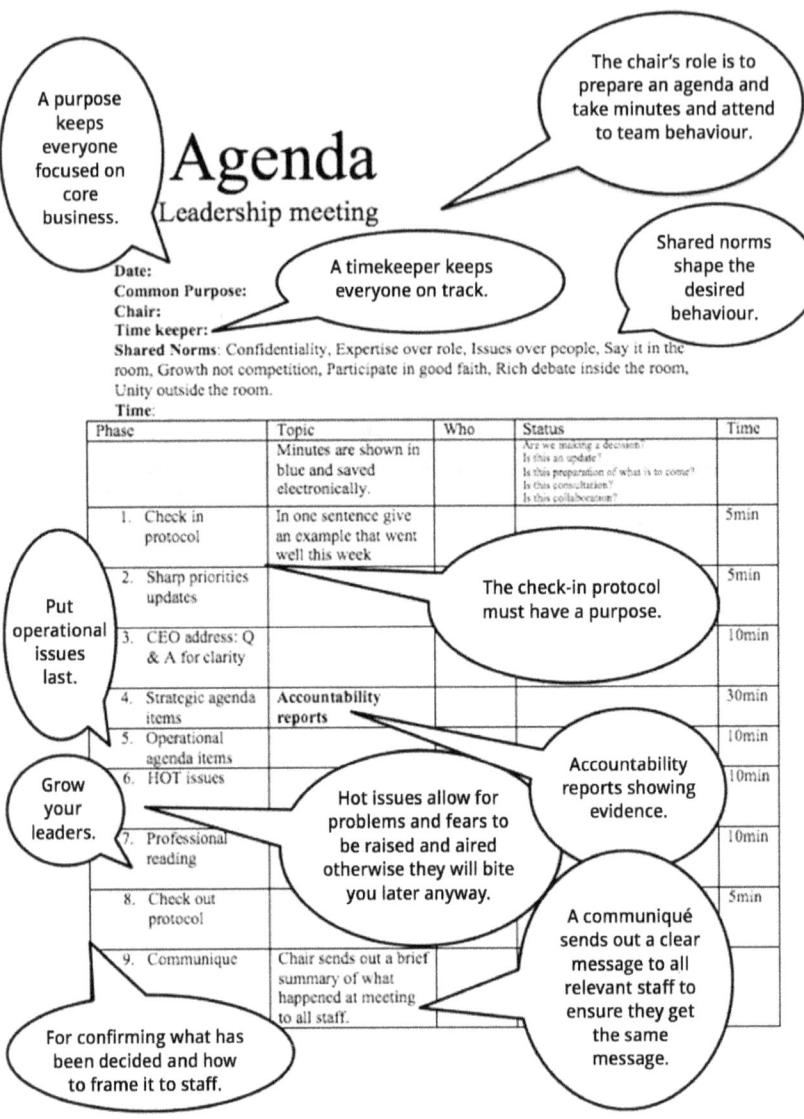

Figure 12: The meeting agenda

Reflective questions

- How can you use the accountability chart to improve communication and decision-making discussions?
- Do your meeting topics go round and round with little time for decisions?
- How can you design your meeting agendas to ensure the strategic leadership work is valued?
- How can you use the accountability chart to keep people working on the important work?
- Can you draw a concept map to show the communication, feedback loops and decision cycles in your school?
- What do you have the authority to say yes to?
- Are you comfortable with saying no so you are free to work on the important work?

L IS FOR LIKEABILITY

'The single most important ingredient in the formula for success is knowing how to get along with people.'
Teddy Roosevelt

We like people who like us

We are more likely to be able to influence others if they look and sound like us. This is more about behaviour standards and social rules than our cultural background or the colour of our skin. Byrne (1971) investigated how similarity in attitudes and interests influences levels of attraction between people. His empirical research found that people were more attracted to others who shared similar attitudes and values with them. Further, people are more attracted to people who like them. This effect can be explained through several mechanisms:

- **Cognitive fluency:** We find it easier and quicker to process incoming data about people who are like us. They feel easier to be around.
- **Perceived similarity:** We feel more comfortable and safer with people who look like us even if the reality is not the case.
- **Social validation:** We validate our own identity when people agree with us and we see ourselves in their eyes. This makes us feel more confident in our beliefs and strengthens the connection with others.

We underestimate how much people like us

In 2016, Epley and Schroeder conducted a study titled 'The truth about liking: What people think they know about others and what they don't', published in the *Journal of Personality and Social Psychology*. This study delved into how people assess their own likeability and the likeability of others, focusing on how self-perception affects social interactions.

The key findings were that we overestimate others' negative impressions when we interact with them. This suggests that we are overly concerned with how people judge us and that we want to be liked. We are focused on our flaws, thinking the other person is doing likewise, but in reality we can blow this out of proportion in our heads. Others are too busy thinking about their own faults. These findings suggest that likeability is more about perception than reality, and if you assume others like you, your likeability tends to increase. The study also found that people who make an effort to understand others and show empathy are rated more likeable. The study underscores that people are more likeable than they think, and their perceptions of themselves can hinder their social success.

> *'What you share with one person will be repeated three more times. How you treat one person gets discussed by many.'*
> Stephen Covey

Reflective questions

- Do you assume that people like you and set aside your fears that might make you appear overly defensive?
- If we put performance over relationships, what challenges does this present?
- How do you have a hard conversation to keep people accountable but keep the relationship intact?
- If we are attracted to people who look and sound like us, what does this mean for recruiting for diversity?

AFTERWORD

INSPIRE – UNITE – DELIVER

Brain 1, our emotional brain, loves certainty, because it makes us feel safe and comfortable. It gives us a sense of control. Don't allow your body language to project your fears and ego; instead lean into challenges, and stay calm to show your strengths and intent. Resist playing small. Put courage over comfort.

Be braver in your leadership to inspire.

Brain 2, our social brain, allows us to touch the feelings of others in heartfelt ways. Reduce the 'them and us' mindset to become one tribe. Connect through love, compassion, optimism, gratitude and hope. See potential and beauty. Project warmth.

Be kinder in your leadership to unite.

Brain 3, our thinking brain, provides the opportunity to learn and achieve. Build credibility and clarity to claim your space. Embrace wonder and curiosity. Go harder and higher.

Be bolder in your leadership to deliver.

Lead from your heart, head and gut, and align your behaviours and words with the physiology, not against it. Leaders are brain changers.

Dr Judi Newman

REFERENCES

Adams, G. S., Converse, B. A., Hales, A. H., & Klotz, L. E. (2021). People systematically overlook subtractive changes. *Nature, 592*(7853), 258-61.

Antonakis, J., Avolio, B. J., & Sivasubramaniam, N. (2011). Context and leadership: An examination of the nine-factor full-range leadership theory and comparisons with transformational and transactional leadership. *The Leadership Quarterly, 22*(6), 1062-85.

Argyris, C., & Schön, D. A. (1974). *Theory in practice: Increasing professional effectiveness.* Jossey-Bass.

Arsten, A. F. T. (2015). Stress weakens prefrontal networks: Molecular results to higher cognition. *Nature Neuroscience, 18*(10), 1376-84.

Avenell, M. (2015). Teachers' preferences for collaborative decision-making in schools: Two Australian studies. *Australian Journal of Education, 59*(1), 65-81.

Avolio, B. J., Walumbwa, F. O., & Weber, T. J. (2009). Leadership: Current theories, research and future directions. *Annual Review of Psychology,* 60, 421-49.

Balthazard, P. A., Waldman, D. A., Thatcher, R. W., & Hannah, S. T. (2012). Differentiating transformational and non-transformational leaders on the basis of neurological imaging. *The Leadership Quarterly, 23,* 244-58.

Bao, S., Chan, U. T., & Merzenich, M. M. (2001). Cortical remodelling induced by activity of ventral tegmental dopamine neurons. *Nature, 412*(6842), 79-83.

Barbuto, J. E., & Burbach, M. E. (2006). The emotional intelligence of transformational leaders: A field study of the impact of leader emotional intelligence on leader effectiveness. *Journal of Leadership & Organizational Studies, 13*(3), 96-108.

Bass, B. M., & Avolio, B. J. (1994). *Improving organizational effectiveness through transformational leadership.* Sage Publications.

Bass, B. M., & Bass, R. (2009). *The Bass handbook of leadership: Theory, research and managerial applications.* (5th Ed.). Free Press.

Bavel, J. J. V., Mende-Siedlecki, P., Brady, W. J., & Van Bavel, C. (2018). Contextual sensitivity in scientific research: A motivational perspective on the relationship between social identity and the interpretation of evidence. *Trends in Cognitive Sciences, 22*(6), 486-98.

Belynder, W. (2024, November 28). *Today choose gratitude.* LinkedIn.

Bennis, W. (2009). *On becoming a leader* (4th ed.). Basic Books.

Blanchard, K. & Johnson, S. (2015). *The new one minute manager.* Williams and Morrow and Company.

Blanchard, K., Oncken, W., Jr., & Burrows, H. (2000). *The one minute manager meets the monkey.* HarperCollins.

Boyatzis, R. (2012). Neuroscience and the link between inspirational leadership and resonant relationships. *Ivey Business Journal.* https://iveybusinessjournal.com/publication/neuroscience-and-the-link-between-inspirational-leadership-and-resonant-relationships-2/

Brebner, D., & Ackroyd, A. (2024). *Living beyond limits: My struggle and triumph over Tourette's syndrome.*

Brewer, M. B,. & Kramer, R. M. (1986). Choice behaviour in social dilemmas: Effects of social identity, group size and decision framing. *Journal of Personality and Social Psychology, 50*(3), 543-49.

Browning, P. (2020). *Principled: 10 leadership practices for building trust.* University of Queensland Press.

Byrne, D. (1971). The influence of interpersonal similarity and liking on interpersonal attraction. *Journal of Personality and Social Psychology, 18*(1), 1-12.

Carmeli, A., Brueller, D., & Dutton, J. E. (2009). Learning behaviours in the workplace: The role of high-quality interpersonal relationships and psychological safety. *Systems Research and Behavioral Science, 26*(1), 81-98.

Cluck, J. A., Peterson, J. E., & Harris, M. A. (2016). Action potentials in neurons: A detailed exploration of mechanisms and physiological roles. *Journal of Neuroscience Research, 44*(2), 130-42.

Collins, J. (2001). *Good to great: Why some companies make the leap... and others don't.* Harper Business.

Cook, S. (2023). *From the ground up: How a community with a vision and a principal with a purpose created a thriving state school.* Black Inc.

Covey, S. (2006). *Speed of trust: The one thing that changes everything.* Simon & Schuster.

Cuddy, A. (2022). ACAP Conference keynote. Sydney.

Cunningham, C. (2014). Decision-making processes and educational leadership in Australia. *Leading and Managing, 20*(1), 11-31.

Damasio, A. R. (1994). *Descartes' error: Emotion, reason, and the human brain.* Putnam Publishing.

Day, S. (2015). *Lessons from the front line.* PwC Australia. http://www.pwc.com.au/publications/the-press/lessons-from-the-front-line.html

Deal, T., & Peterson, K. (2016). Shaping school culture. Jossey-Bass.

Decety, J., & Michaiska, K. J. (2010). Neurodevelopmental change in circuits underlying empathy and sympathy from childhood to adulthood. *Developmental Science 13*(6), 886-99.

Dimoka, (2010). What does the brain tell us about trust and distrust? Evidence from a functional neuroimaging study. *MIS Quarterly, 34*(2), 373-77.

Dunbar, R. I. M. (1992). Neocortex size as a constraint on group size in primates. *Journal of Human Evolution, 22*(6), 469-93.

Dweck, C. (2006). *Mindset: The new psychology of success.* Random House.

Edelman, G. M. (1987). *Neural Darwinism: The theory of neuronal group selection.* Basic Books.

Edmondson, A. (1999). Psychological safety and learning behaviour in work teams. *Administrative Science Quarterly, 44*(2), 350-83.

Edmondson, A. (2019). *The fearless organisation: Creating psychological safety in the workplace for learning, innovation and growth.* John Wiley & Sons.

Eisenberger, N. I. (2012). The pain of social disconnection: Examining the shared neural underpinnings of physical and social pain. *Nature Reviews Neuroscience, 13*, 421-34.

Epley, N., & Schroeder, J. (2016). The truth about liking: What people think they know about others and what they don't. *Journal of Personality and Social Psychology, 110*(5), 622-40.

Fehr, B., Samsom., D., & Paulhus, D. L. (1992). The construct of Machiavellianism: Twenty years later. In C. D. Spielberger & J. N. Butcher (Eds.), *Advances in personality assessment*, Vol. 9, pp. 77-116. Lawrence Erlbaum Associates, Inc.

Feser, C. (2016). *When execution isn't enough: Decoding inspirational leadership.* Wiley.

Fiske, S., Cuddy, A. J. C., Glick, P., & Xu, J. (2002). A model of (often mixed) stereotype content: Competence and warmth respectively follow from perceived status and competition. *Journal of Personality and Social Psychology, 82*(6), 878–902.

Frederickson, B. L. (2011). The role of positive emotions in positive psychology: The broaden and build theory of positive emotions. *American Psychologist, 56*, 218–26.

Friedman, R. S., & Förster, J. (2001). The effects of promotion and prevention cues on creativity. *Journal of Personality and Social Psychology, 81*(6), 1001–1013.

Froemke, K., Merzenich, M. M., & Schiener, C. E. (2007). A synaptic memory trace for cortical receptive field plasticity, *Nature, 450*(7168), 425–29.

Gage, N. (1989). *The teacher who changed my life.* New York Times.

Gallo, C. (2011). Richard Branson: The one skill leaders need to learn. *Forbes.* https://www.forbes.com/sites/carminegallo/2011/06/29/richard-branson-the-one-skill-leaders-need-to-learn/

Garrett, N., Lazzaro, S. C., Ariely, D., & Sharot, T. (2016). The brain adapts to dishonesty. *Nature Neuroscience, 19*, 1727–32.

Gino, F. (2018). The business case for curiosity. *Harvard Business Review.* https://hbr.org/2018/09/the-business-case-for-curiosity

Glasser, W. (1998). *Choice theory: A new psychology of personal freedom.* Harper Perennial.

Gluck, M. A., Mercado, E., & Myers, C. E. (2016). *Learning and memory: From brain to behavior* (3rd ed.). Worth Publishers.

Goldberg, M. C. (1998). *The art of the question: A guide to short-term question-centered therapy.* Wiley.

Goleman, D. (2013). The focused leader. *Harvard Business Review.* https://hbr.org/2013/12/the-focused-leader

Goleman, D. (2019). *Emotional intelligence: Why it can matter more than IQ* (25th anniversary ed.). Bantam.

Goman, C. K. (2011). *The silent language of leaders: How body language can help – or hurt – how you lead.* Jossey-Bass.

Good, K., & Shaw, A. (2022). Being curious versus appearing smart: Children's developing intuitions about how reputational motives guide behaviour. *Child Development, 93*(2), 418–36.

Gordon, E., (2020, March 26). 20 Key brain questions. [Audio podcast]. *Total Brain.* https://www.buzzsprout.com/735944/episodes/3182671-20-key-brain-questions-dr-evian-gordon-phd-md

Gordon, E. (2022). *From knowing to doing.* Franklin Publishing.

Gordon, E., Cooper, N., Rennie, C., Hermens, D., & Williams, L. M. (2008). An integrative neuroscience platform: Application to profiles of negativity and positivity bias. *Journal of Integrative Neuroscience, 7*(3), 345–66.

Grant, A. M. (2013). The significance of appreciation in the workplace. *Journal of Applied Psychology, 98*(2), 332–44.

Hackel, L. M., Zaki, J., & Van Bavel, J. J. (2017). Social identity shapes social valuation: Evidence from prosocial behavior and vicarious reward. *Social Cognitive and Affective Neuroscience, 12*(8), 1219–28.

Hackman, M. Z., & Johnson, C. E. (2009). *Leadership: A communication perspective* (5th ed.). Waveland Press.

Hanson, R. (2015, August 7). Using your mind to change your brain. https://rickhanson.com/using-your-mind-to-change-your-brain/

Hanson, R., & Mendius, R. (2009). *Buddha's brain: The practical neuroscience of happiness, love & wisdom.* New Harbinger Publications.

Harter J. (2024, January 23). In new workplace, U.S. employee engagement stagnates. *Gallup*. https://www.gallup.com/workplace/608675/new-workplace-employee-engagement-stagnates.aspx

Haslam, S. A., & Platow, M. J. (2001). The link between leadership and followship: How affirming social identify translates vision into action. *Personality and Social Psychology Bulletin, 27*, 1469–79.

Haslam, S. A., Reicher, S. D., & Platow, M. J. (2013). *The new psychology of leadership identity, influence and power*. Psychology Press.

Henley, D. (2022). This leadership trait goes a long way, *Forbes*. https://www.forbes.com/sites/dedehenley/2022/06/26/this-leadership-trait-goes-a-long-way/?sh=6440d98a7e9b

Hills, J. (2014). Are your leaders brain savvy and why you should know. *Strategic HR Review, 13*(1), 11–15.

Holt-Lunstad, J. (2017). So lonely I could die. *American Psychological Association*. https://www.apa.org/news/press/releases/2017/08/lonely-die

Holt-Lunstad, J., Smith, T. B., Baker, M., Harris, T., & Stephenson, D. (2015). Loneliness and social isolation as risk factors for mortality: A meta-analytic review. *Perspectives on Psychological Science, 10*(2), 227–37.

Horwitch, M., & Whipple-Callahan, M. (2016, June 9). How leaders inspire: Cracking the code. *Bain & Company*. https://www.bain.com/insights/how-leaders-inspire-cracking-the-code/

Immordino-Yang, M. H., Yang, X., & Damasio, H. (2016). Cultural modes of expressing emotions influence how emotions are expressed. *Emotion, 16*(7), 1033–39.

Jung-Beeman, M., Collier, A., & Kounios, J. (2008). How insight happens: Learning from the brain. *Neuroleadership Journal, 1*, 26–33.

Kahneman, D. (2011). *Thinking, fast and slow*. Penguin Books.

Kahneman, D., Sibony, O., & Sunstein, C. R. (2021). *Noise: A flaw in human judgment*. Little, Brown and Company.

Kaiser, K., & Young, S. D. (2013). *The blue line imperative: A radical new approach to value-based leadership*. Jossey-Bass.

Kandel, E. R. (2012). *The age of content: The quest to understand the unconscious in art, mind and brain*. Random House.

Karpman, S. B. (1968). Fairy tales and script drama analysis. *Transactional Analysis Bulletin, 7*(26), 39–43.

Kellerman, B. (2012). *The end of leadership*. Harper Business.

Keltner, D. (2017). *The power paradox: How we gain and lose influence*. Penguin.

Kennedy. J. J. (2021). Build a resilient brain: A webinar with Dr. Justin James Kennedy. *The Upside*. https://www.happify.com/hd/build-a-resilient-brain-with-doctor-justin-james-kennedy-webinar/

Kirby, J. (2019, December 3). Cited in Kesteven, S., The chemistry and psychology of kindness,*ABCLife*.https://www.abc.net.au/news/2019-12-03/the-science-behind-the-warm-glow-of-kindness/11749268

Kirsten, J. (2007). Cited in Nelson, C. A., Zeanah, C. H., Fox, N. A., Marshall, P. J., & Smyke, A. T. Cognitive recovery in socially deprived young children: The Bucharest Early Intervention Project. *Science, 318*(5858), 1937–40.

Korn Ferry. (n.d.). *Enterprise leadership: New leadership for a new world*. Retrieved July 4, 2025, from https://www.kornferry.com/insights/featured-topics/leadership/enterprise-leadership-framework

Kouzes, J., M., & Posner, B. Z. (1990). The credibility factor: What followers expect from their leaders. *Management Review, 79*(1), 29–33.

Krasikova, D. V., Green, S. G., & Lebreton, J. M. (2013). Destructive leadership: A theoretical review, integration and future research agenda. *Journal of Management, 39,* 1308–38.

Kruger, F., McCabe, K., Moll, J., Kriegeskorte, N., Zahn, R., Strenziok, N., Heinecke, A., & Grafman, J. (2007). Neural correlates of trust. *Proceedings of the National Academy of Sciences, 104* (50), 20084–89.

Kübler-Ross, E. (1969). *On death and dying: What the dying have to teach doctors, nurses, clergy and their own families.* Scribner.

Lambruschini, S. L. (2016). *The connection spectrum: How leaders experience interpersonal connection in the workplace.* [Thesis Dissertation, California Institute of Integral Studies.]

LeDoux, J. (2002). *Synaptic self: How our brains become who we are.* Viking.

Levin, M. (2017, March 30). Why great leaders (like Richard Branson) inspire instead of motivate. *Inc.* https://www.inc.com/marissa-levin/why-great-leaders-like-richard-branson-inspire-instead-of-motivate.html

Levine, L. E., & Murnane, J. (2012). The Lego bias: How adults are biased toward adding rather than subtracting in problem solving. *Journal of Behavioural Decision Making, 25*(2), 173–79.

Lieberman, M. D. (2007). Social cognitive neuroscience: A review of core processes. *Annual Review of Psychology, 58,* 259–89.

Locklear, L. R., Taylor, S. G., & Ambrose, M. L. (2020, November 27). Building a better workplace starts with saying 'thanks'. *Harvard Business Review, 39*(1).

MacKinnon, L. (2012). The neurosequential model of therapeutics: An interview with Bruce Perry. *Australian and New Zealand Journal of Family Therapy, 33*(3), 210–18.

McCraty, R., & Shaffer, F. (2023). Heart rate variability: New perspectives on physiological mechanisms, assessment of self-regulatory capacity, and health risk. *Global Advances in Health and Medicine, 4*(1), 46–61.

Medina. J. (2008). *Brain rules.* Scribe Publications.

Men, L. R. (2014). The effects of leadership communication on employee outcomes: A study of Chinese employees in state-owned enterprises. *Journal of Business Communication, 51*(4), 398–418.

Molenberghs, P., Prochilo, P., Steffens, N. K., Zacher, H., & Haslam, S. A. (2015). The neuroscience of inspirational leadership: The importance of collective-oriented language and shared group membership. *Journal of Management, 43*(7), 1–27.

Nelson, C. A., Zeanah, C. H., Fox, N. A., Marshall, P. J., Smyke, A. T., & Guthrie, D. (2007). Cognitive recovery in socially deprived young children: The Bucharest Early Intervention Project. *Science, 318*(5858), 1937–2940.

Newman, J. (2010). *The Okojo Protocol.* The Academy of Organisational Neuroscience (AONA).

Newman, J. (2020). *The 18 trust behaviours.* The Academy of Organisational Neuroscience (AONA).

Newman, J. (2022). *What are the attributes of inspirational leadership? A case study of principals of four large high schools.* [PhD Thesis, Central Queensland University.]

Nobre, M. T. R., & Martins, F. M. G. (2021). Accountability in decision-making: A meta-analytic review. *Personality and Social Psychology Bulletin, 47*(2), 145–63.

Northouse, P. G. (2018). *Leadership: Theory and practice* (8th ed.). SAGE Publications.

Ochsner, K. N., & Lieberman, M. D. (2001). The emergence of social cognitive neuroscience. *American Psychologist, 56*(9), 717–34.

Parker, K. E., Pedersen, C. E., Gomez, A. M., Dougherty, J. D., Stuber, G. D., & Bruchas, M. R. (2019). A paranigral VTA nociceptin circuit that constrains motivation for reward. *Cell, 178*(3), 653–71.

Payne, R. K. (2005). *A framework for understanding poverty* (4th ed.). Aha! Process, Inc.

Rhoades, L., & Eisenberger, R. (2002). Perceived organisational support: A review of the literature. *Journal of Applied Psychology, 87*(4), 698–714.

Richmond-Rakerd, L. S., Caspi, A., Ambler, A., d'Arbeloff, T., de Bruine, M., Elliott, M., Harrington, H. L., Hogan, S., Houts, R. M., Ireland, D., Keenan, R., Knodt, A. R., Melzer, T. R., Park, S., Poulton, R., Ramrakha, S., Rasmussen, L. J. H., Sack, E., Schmidt, A. T., Sison, M. L., Wertz, J., Hariri, A. R., & Moffitt, T. E. (2021). Childhood self-control forecasts the pace of midlife aging and preparedness for old age. *Proceedings of the National Academy of Sciences, 118*(3), e2010211118.

Rilling, J. K., Gutman, D., Zeh, T., Pagnoni, G., Berns, G., & Kilts, C. (2002). A neural basis for social cooperation. *Neuron, 35*(2), 395–405.

Robinson, V. M. J., Lloyd, C., & Rowe, K. J. (2008). The impact of leadership on student outcomes: An analysis of the differential effects of leadership types. *Education Administration Quarterly, 44*(5), 635–74.

Rock, D. (2008). SCARF: A brain-based model for collaborating with and influencing others. *Neuroleadership Journal, 1*, 44-52.

Sample, M. (2024). *Being teachable is our path to success!* LinkedIn. https://www.linkedin.com/feed/update/urn:li:activity:7241252265783668737?utm_source=share&utm_medium=member_desktop&rcm=ACoAAAIfJLIB6EEVP9WEzEABpJsNkEQE2KAHkLo

Sapolsky, R. M. (2004). *Why zebras don't get ulcers: The acclaimed guide to stress, stress-related diseases, and coping* (3rd ed.). Henry Holt and Company.

Schaufenbuel, K. (2014). *The Neuroscience of leadership: Practical applications*. UNC.

Schein, E. H. (2010). *Organizational culture and leadership* (4th ed.). Jossey-Bass.

Schwantes, M. (2025, May 22). Shifting workplace cultures, Linkedin.

Scott, S. (2010). *Fierce conversations: Achieving success at work and in life one conversation at a time*. Penguin.

Senge, P. (Ed). (2000). *Schools that learn: A fifth discipline fieldbook for educators, parents, and everyone who cares about education*. Doubleday.

Sergiovanni, T. (2004). Collaborative cultures and communities of practice. *Principal Leadership, 5*(1), 48–52.

Sinek, S. (2024, November 19). *How to make others feel like they matter*. The Optimism Company.

Smith, A. R., & Jones, B. T. (2021). The impact of leadership strength on team performance. *Journal of Leadership and Organizational Studies, 28*(3), 245–60.

Stebbins, P. (2015). Workshop: High Performance Schools, Department of Education.

Steffens, K. N., & Haslam, S. A. (2013). Power through 'us': Leaders' use of we-referencing language predicts election victory. *PLoS ONE 8*(10): e77952.

Storoni M. (2024, September 5). *The hidden health dangers of stress. Simple Scaling*. YouTube. https://www.youtube.com/watch?v=hNKoM7Q5Nr8

Surowiecki, J. (2004). *The wisdom of crowds: Why the many are smarter than the few and how collective wisdom shapes business, economies, societies, and nations*. Doubleday & Co.

Swart, T., Chrisholm, K., & Brown, P. (2015). *Neuroscience for leadership: Harnessing the brain gain advantage*. Palgrave Macmillan.

Thaler, R. H., & Sunstein, C. R. (2022). *Nudge: Improving decisions about health, wealth and happiness*. Penguin.

Thomas, B. C., Croft, K. E., & Tranel, D. (2011). Harming kin to save strangers: Further evidence for abnormally utilitarian moral judgments after ventromedial prefrontal damage. *Journal of Cognitive Neuroscience, 23*(9), 2186–96.

Tracy, B. (2017). *Eat that frog! 21 great ways to stop procrastinating and get more done in less time*. Berrett-Koehler.

Tressel, J. (2001). Cited in Van Bavel, J. J., Packer, D. J., Payne, C., & Rock, D. (2018). The neuroscience of leading effective teams. *Neuroleadership Journal*, (7), 5-15.

Ultimate Software. (2017). *The state of employee engagement: A study on what drives employee engagement and why it matters*. Ultimate Software.

Van Bavel, J. J. & Packer, D. (2016, December 28). The problem with rewarding individual performers. *Harvard Business Review*. https://hbr.org/2016/12/the-problem-with-rewarding-individual-performers

Waldman, D. A., Balthazard, P. A., & Peterson, S. J. (2011). Leadership and neuroscience: Can we revolutionise the way that inspirational leaders are identified and developed? *Academy of Management Perspectives, 25*(1), 60-74.

Wang, J. R., & Hsieh, S. (2013). Neurofeedback training improves attention and working memory performance. *Clinical Neurophysiology, 124*(12), 2406-20.

Wang, Y. (2019). Pulling at your heart strings: Examining four leadership approaches from the neuroscience perspective. *Educational Administration Quarterly, 55*(2), 328-59.

Washington Post. (2016, December 8). Leaders are more powerful when they're humble, new research shows. *Inspired Life*. https://www.washingtonpost.com/news/inspired-life/wp/2016/12/08/leaders-are-more-powerful-when-theyre-humble-new-research-shows/

Weir K. (2014). The lasting impact of neglect. *Monitor on Psychology, 45*(6).

Whitman, G., & Kelleher, I. (2016). *Neuroteach: Brain science and the future of education*. Rowman & Littlefield.

Wicker, B., Keysers, C., Plailly, J., Royet, J., Gallese, V., & Rizzolatti, G. (2003). Both of us disgusted in my insula: The common neural basis of seeing and feeling disgust. *Neuron, 40*(3), 655-64.

Willink, J., & Babin, L. (2017). *Extreme ownership: How US Navy seals lead and win*. St. Martin's Press.

Willis, J. (2016). Stepping up social-emotional learning to reignite all brains. *Kappa Delta Pi Record, 57*(1), 18-22.

Willis, J. (2020). Author interview with Dr Judy Willis, 1 July 2019, CQUniversity.

Wilson, T. D. (2002). *Strangers to ourselves: Discovering the adaptive unconscious*. Harvard University Press.

Xu, J., & Cooper Thomas, H. (2011). How can leaders achieve high employee engagement? *Leadership and Organisation Development Journal, 32*(4), 333-416.

Zak, P. J. (2022). *Immersion: The science of the extraordinary and the source of happiness*. Lioncrest Publishing.

Zaki, J., & Ochsner, K. (2012). The neuroscience of empathy: Progress, pitfalls and promises. *Focus on Social Neuroscience, 15*, 675-80.

www.ingramcontent.com/pod-product-compliance
Lightning Source LLC
Chambersburg PA
CBHW052024070526
44584CB00016B/1883